HELPING PEOPLE WITH DISABILITIES HELP THEMSELVES
Promoting the I CAN Attitude

by

Barbara Jean Young

authorHOUSE™

1663 LIBERTY DRIVE, SUITE 200
BLOOMINGTON, INDIANA 47403
(800) 839-8640
WWW.AUTHORHOUSE.COM

First published by AuthorHouse 01/10/05

ISBN: 1-4208-8758-0 (sc)
ISBN: 1-4208-8757-2 (dj)

Printed in the United States of America
Bloomington, Indiana

This book is printed on acid-free paper.

Acknowledgments

I would like to thank my family for the support, love, and guidance they have given me while writing this book. My mother and father, Robert and Colette Lorenzen, have taught me to look at all people and find beauty in them. My photograph was taken by my sister, Linda Hoernke. My husband, Kelly Young; my father, Robert Lorenzen; and my sister, Linda Hoernke, spent many hours reading, suggesting, and reinforcing my work. My brother, Bob Lorenzen, and my mother, Colette Lorenzen, gave me the love and support which I needed to keep writing until I had completed this book.

Table of Contents

Introduction

Waking up one morning, I found myself in strange surroundings. I noticed my bed was surrounded by railings. I noticed a calendar hanging on the wall. The calendar read March 1976, and three weeks were marked off. Confusion set in as I had just started my last semester at the University of Arizona, which meant the date should have read January. In the distance I heard someone saying Barbara Jean is awake. Call the doctor. I tried to get out of bed, but my right arm and leg would not budge. Once again I heard my name being called out. I noticed a man approaching my bed. He introduced himself as my neurosurgeon.

Concentrating on what the doctor was saying was very difficult as I went in and out of consciousness. He began describing a horrendous automobile accident I was in. I was driving home from my evening job as a mental retardation specialist at an institution for people who have mental retardation. A drunken driver ran a stop sign and collided into the right side of my small car. My car crumpled down on top of me. I became unconscious. Jaws of life were used to pry my mangled body out of the car. CPR was immediately used as I was not breathing. The paramedics rushed my battered body to the University of Arizona Medical Center. I had been in a coma for two and a half months. I was on life support for two months. There was severe damage to the left side of my brain. I had severe neurological damage, causing right side paralysis.

My right shoulder blade and four vertebras were damaged. My right inner ear, which controls balance was injured. I had vocal chord paralysis. I was then told I would be paralyzed on the right side and would never be able to walk again. The realization hit me that I may be wheel chair bound for the rest of my life. I tried to speak expressing my concern over the situation I was in, but no words came out. Noticing my frustration, my neurosurgeon said I also had vocal chord paralysis and would be unable to speak. Since I had known deaf sign language, I tried to sign describing the pain I was in. That was a very difficult feat, as I had problems remembering most words in sign language. Not remembering the majority of sign was very irritating as I was fluent in sign language prior to the accident. Also with my right side paralysis, I had no movement in my right fingers, hand, and arms. I was in total disbelief about the extreme change in my life.

Prior to the accident, I worked with a variety of people with disabilities. The majority of my work was with the people who are hearing impaired, have mental disabilities and emotional disabilities. I taught adults and children who were nonverbal to express themselves by using sign language. The realization came to me that I now had mental and physical disabilities similar to the people I had dedicated my life to. All my dreams and goals of eventually supervising my own clinic for people who had disabilities had now become unattainable. My life now was filled with uncertainties. At the thought of these circumstances, tears began rolling down my face. At that moment I noticed my father, Bob Lorenzen, walking into the room. In his caring, direct, and loving manner he stated that I had physical and even mental disabilities but with determination I would be able to handle all the obstacles presented to me. He convinced me that I needed to address each problem as they arose. Along with love and support from my friends and especially my family, help from a remarkable therapist team, excellent medical staff, prayers, hypnosis, and developing the "I Can" attitude, I overcame many physical and mental obstacles. I made unexpected and remarkable progress.. The continuous support from my family was the primary reason for my progress. While I was in a coma, my parents, Bob and Colette Lorenzen; my brother, Robert Lorenzen; and my sister, Linda Hoernke spent shifts, on a twenty-four basis, speaking to me of the positive happenings in my life. I also received support from the adolescents who had mental disabilities that I had supervised. In small groups, they were allowed to visit me in intensive care. Encouragement and support gave me the motivation that I will survive and overcome all the challenges presented to me. I then knew I would continue my work with all disabilities. I had a better understanding of trails and tribulations of people with disabilities since now I had disabilities.

The challenges I had to address were numerous. Although I relearned to speak, I now had a speech deficiency. My speech pattern was slow and my syntax would become jumbled at times. This became more apparent when I felt I was under pressure to express or explain myself, or when I was tired or stressed. This caused many looks and crude remarks. My physical slowness or lack of coordination also brought negative attention. Regardless of people's negativity toward my disabilities, I succeeded beyond all expectations. Through determination, prayer and the use of the "I Can" attitude, I learned to walk, talk, and think once again. I completed my bachelor's degree in special education in 1980, with a certification in teaching people with mental disabilities.

Within the next six years I became certified in teaching learning disabilities, emotional disabilities, physical disabilities and teaching sign language in junior colleges. In the middle 80's, I obtained my certifications in hypnotherapy, specializing in four areas. This was all possible because of the "I Can" attitude.

From 1980-2000, I taught school in various settings ranging from public schools, a school for the deaf, a mental institution, and a detention center. During the evenings and weekends, I worked with families of children from birth to five years old who are deaf, blind, or have multiple disabilities. I also had a lucrative hypnosis business. I worked all these various jobs to motivate people that had either physical or mental problems. With my support and example, that they too can succeed in their goals and aspirations. I also had a need to prove to myself that I can independently function and succeed at my life long dream of working with a variety of disabilities. Because of having disabilities, I had the opportunity to meet the challenges of and respond to many people with disabilities that they too can succeed by using the "I Can" attitude despite obstacles. Their dreams then could also be a reality.

I am now retired. Through the MADD (Mothers Against Drunk Drivers) organization, I speak to drivers in Arizona who were ticketed for DUI. I tell them about the possible consequences of driving under the influence. I speak in detail about my accident and the difficulties of having disabilities.

This book is written to introduce people to the world of disabilities. By encouraging and promoting the "I Can" attitude during interaction with people who have disabilities, many of their obstacles can be overcome.

Chapter 1

UNDERSTANDING AND RELATING TO PEOPLE WITH DISABILITIES

The primary attitude toward people displaying certain traits of a disability is still basically negative. People tend to overreact, criticize, or make fun of the inability to perform in a "normal" set of patterns. As a special education teacher, I often went with my students on outings or field trips. We were often met with stares, finger pointing, rude comments, ridiculing, or even mimicking of the mental or physical impairments or behaviors.

Rude remarks or behaviors usually have a psychological effect upon the persons with disabilities. This is reflective of the time I was with a group of people with mental disabilities in a state van. The state van was clearly marked with the symbol of the mental retardation training program where the clients resided. Stopped at a traffic light, the people in the car adjacent to us began making faces and yelling out rude comments. Victor, an adolescent in the van, yelled out the window, "You retard!" He had heard this phrase so many times that he thought the phrase was a derogatory comment to demean all people. A few of the higher functioning people in the van became upset over why they were constantly the subject of ridicule.

This incident, combined with many similar ones, resulted in feelings of failure and hopelessness. Ridiculing causes many people not to try because they believe what they have heard and experienced. They develop negative attitudes and are convinced that they cannot achieve many things. Regardless of the age or skill I was trying to teach, the usual comment I would hear in the beginning was "I can't." After continually being reminded that "I can't" was a phrase which was not allowed, attitudes changed. Many of my students would inform a new student that they should not say "I can't" or there would be consequences. By prohibiting that one small phrase, unbelievable progress was made.

When given the "I Can" attitude with support and love, an individual can progress both physically and mentally despite the negative reactions toward his/her disabilities. An important fact to remember is that people with disabilities are people, too. Their feelings can be hurt just like any other individual. Positive involvement with a person who has disabilities makes a huge difference in their outlook on life and progression toward needed goals. Modeling, encouraging people with disabilities to respond, and mimicking positive behaviors builds strong personalities. Positive behaviors can be learned and strengthened by the following methods:

a) Praise people with disabilities in areas that they have attempted and accomplished.

b) Spend quality time doing activities they enjoy.

c) Show love and compassion.

d) Treat all people, regardless of the circumstances or disabilities, with respect. Put yourself in the place of the person with disabilities.

e) Resolve all problems peacefully and in a direct manner.

f) Work together on different daily living skills, i.e., dressing or eating appropriately.

g) Make learning a fun project.

h) Relate learning experiences to everyday living.

i) Give consistent and honest messages.

These methods should be applied regardless of the person's disability or intellectual capacity.

When a child or an adult with a disability is outside of their living environment, three major factors are extremely important to stress. Physical appearance is very important for first impressions. Basic social skills including manners and politeness are essential for interaction. Appropriate behaviors and communication determined by the place and the people involved are crucial.

Instilling the "I Can" attitude will make a difference in the way one is perceived by others. When I ventured out into the city with a group, I always emphasized the importance of behavior, appearance, and especially attitude. There is less reaction from people in society when the people with disabilities are able to blend in.

One young adolescent with mental disabilities, called Suzi, whom I worked with in an institution, had no academic skills, no communication skills, no self-help skills, and no social skills. Suzy's only form of communication was through aggression. She acquired these aggressive tendencies because from infancy on, she had to defend herself because of a lack of supervision in her life. Suzy's only forms of communication were yelling, hitting, biting, kicking, and pulling hair. After many months of one-to-one training reinforced by using the positive approach and educating her with the "I Can" attitude, she accomplished more than what was ever expected. She improved in self-help, behavior, communication, social skills, and even in primary academics.

Regardless of how simple a task may seem to the majority of people, that task may be very difficult for someone who may not have been trained in the basics or has a physical disability which impedes that person from performing the task. With compassion, time, and the "I Can" attitude, a person can achieve many different tasks. Putting oneself in the place of the person with disabilities will promote understanding of the frustrations of having difficulty in completing a specific task. With patience, and if need be, manual guidance, the person with disabilities will be able to learn basic skills.

John, an adult with mental disabilities, could not tie his shoes. I began placing his hands on the shoestrings. I placed my hands on top of his. With manual guidance, he learned this basic skill. I put the tying of shoes into simple steps and then gradually phased away from manual guidance as John independently completed each step. After several months, John eventually learned this skill. With great pride, he untied and tied his shoes for everybody who came in contact with him.

Prior to developing the "I Can" attitude, a very scared adolescent with mental disabilities, called Mary, fought taking showers. I placed a washcloth in her hand, showed her how to the glide the soap on the washcloth, and manually guided her on the techniques of washing herself. We started with her arms and face. From there, Mary understood the concept and I phased away from the manual guidance. I then used a separate washcloth and modeled areas on me that should be washed. With encouragement, Mary mimicked my motions, washing all areas of her body. She began accomplishing this task independently. When she was cleaned and dried off, I reinforced her by smiling and over-exaggerating how pretty she looked. After Mary was dressed, she saw herself in a mirror and was very pleased. I took pictures of her before and after she was appropriately groomed and dressed. We then placed both pictures on her locker. After that, there was no problem at shower times.

To reinforce Mary's newly acquired skills; we went to a restaurant in the city. Prior to our restaurant visit, we made a communication book. I placed pictures of foods and drinks on each page along with the word printed underneath each picture. I taught her sign language and speech for each picture. I paired each picture with the actual item and with the item listed on a menu. Using this method,

Mary became proficient and at ease "reading" a menu. I showed her pictures of both the inside and outside of the restaurant where we would eat. She then understood the concept. The day of the restaurant trip, I bought her a dress. This was the first time in her life that Mary wore a dress. I shampooed and styled her hair.

Before we left the institution, I showed her the pictures of the inside and outside of the restaurant and told her that we were going there to eat. When Mary saw the front of the restaurant and matched the picture to the actual place, she became very excited. Walking into the restaurant, her face lit up and she had a smile from ear to ear. She was just like other people. When we sat down at the table and were handed the menu, Mary placed her communication book next to the menu. I once again demonstrated to her how the words in the menu compared to the words in her book. After asking Mary what she wanted to eat and drink, she pointed to items in her picture book and attempted to voice the word along with a sign. We then compared the word underneath the picture to the menu. When the waitress arrived at the table, this challenged child was able to order by herself by pointing to the items and attempting to say what she wanted.

During that time, Mary demonstrated many positive academic, social, and behavioral skills. She even signed and attempted to say thank you when the food was brought to her. She was very happy and proud that she was able to independently order food and sit in a public place without being the center of negative attention from other people in the restaurant.

From then on, Mary improved miraculously in all areas. Without the concept of "I Can" and without showing her love, care, and compassion, she would have never succeeded.

Awareness that a person has a possibility of being diagnosed either with disabilities that are physical, mental, social, or emotional is indicated by a series of characteristics or behaviors displayed over a period of time. Documentation along with observation and testing may indicate a need for special education services in the following areas: autism, emotional disability, hearing impairment, other health impairments, a specific learning disability, mental disability at the levels of mild, moderate, and severe; multiple disability, multiple disability with severe sensory impairments, orthopedic impairment, preschool speech/language delay or impairment, traumatic brain injury, or visual impairment.[1] The basic areas of deficiencies that are addressed within these disabilities are cognitive, behavioral, social, emotional, or physical.[2]

Areas that indicate a possible problem in the cognitive realm are inattentiveness, extreme difficulties and signs of frustration while working on age-appropriate tasks and skills, distractibility to the task at hand, refusal to attend to the task, daydreaming, becoming "ill" when questioned or given age-appropriate materials, not finishing work despite trying to accomplish the task, and responding with inappropriate or illogical answers. If the person is not identified and not given appropriate materials and

---

[1] Arizona Center for Disability Law. *Educational Rights for Students with Disabilities.* 6/11/01, p.10.

[2] Edward Zuckman *Clinician's Thesaurus.* 1995, p.92.

tasks, he/she will refuse to try and either become quiet and sullen or be rowdy. This is the cause of falling further behind cognitively as well as emotionally and socially. In many cases, the person with disabilities feels embarrassed to receive special help while the other students or workers can succeed without the need for intervention. They will try to seek any type of attention whether it is negative or positive. A good example is children with disabilities, ages nine to seventeen, whom I taught in a detention center. These children suffered the consequences of being rejected by peers, some guardians, and society in general. Acceptance was found from gang members or the other problematic people in society. Because of the need to be accepted, they complied with demands of troubled people regardless of the punishments for their negative behaviors. These behaviors and consequences affected their ability to progress.

An open and honest discussion with the person who is labeled or displays unacceptable traits is extremely important. Listening to feelings concerning problems will assist the individual in dealing with the facts. Guiding him through his emotions about not functioning like others and not meeting the expectations of society will assist him in solving his problems. Recognition that all people need assistance at one time or another and needing assistance should not be the cause of embarrassment is extremely important concepts to stress. It is imperative to have the person become aware that, even though he may be compared to his classmates negatively or that the time for learning or completing various tasks may vary from his classmates, he is still an okay person. With using the "I Can" attitude, he will be able to succeed. This concept is the basis for succeeding in all areas of life.

One adolescent with emotional and mental disabilities whom I taught in a detention center had very little knowledge of reading, writing, or arithmetic. He was incarcerated for committing a heinous crime. In a few months, he learned to read basic words, especially the survival words, learned basic addition and subtraction, and was able to print his name. By learning basic academics, his whole outlook on life changed. His aggressive tendencies were being replaced with logical and appropriate behaviors.

Many public schools now have all children with disabilities included in the regular classroom with the support of a special education teacher or teacher's aide for a specific amount of time. Success in the cognitive area for students with disabilities is dependent upon many factors. Included in this set are the frequency and type of reinforcement, materials adapted to the needs of the student with disabilities, the basic school attitude toward relating to special needs, and reactions from people who come in contact with the person with disabilities including parents, other students, the regular classroom teacher, and the special education teacher. Prior to a student with disabilities being placed in a regular classroom, a discussion with the other students in the class about the disability of the student will have a positive effect upon the acceptance and the work of the student with disabilities.

In a few schools where I taught, I was permitted to speak to a class that would host the student with disabilities. The students of the classes asked logical questions about the disability. Through this interaction, the child with disabilities was accepted into the classes and several students were even willing to assist with academics.

The parents, guardians, or friends should support and listen to the frustrations which develop in attempting to accomplish difficult tasks. Being able to express one's self and talk out problems will aid in improving the mental as well as emotional capacity. A strong foundation for achieving success in the cognitive realm is built on developing self-esteem through the concept of "I Can".

Behaviors that should be addressed are any type of substance abuse, behaviors stemming from self-abusiveness or from abusing others, aggressiveness, speech difficulties, over- or under-excitement, wording or changes in volume of the voice, odd movements of the body, sexual preoccupation, and adverse physical or mental reactions toward people and situations. Keeping a baseline or record on the frequencies and circumstances which bring about the behavior will assist in targeting the problem.

A study of the effects of medication that is given will indicate if the behavior is medically induced. If indicated, a change in medications may be advised or behavioral plans need to be written that deal with the noted effects. The primary step in alleviating a behavioral problem is confronting the individual about his problem. Lead and guide the person to discover acceptable alternatives to deal with the problem. Having the person be part of the solution will facilitate in eradicating an aversive behavior. In dealing with any disability, I would guide the person to develop a plan to deal with unwanted behaviors.

Trust and respect are major elements in alleviating behavior problems. Trust may not immediately be evident. Once built, trust will aid the person to accomplish many tasks. Being trusted in developing solutions for alleviating the behavioral problem will assist them in claiming responsibility and ownership for the problem. People who have been mentally or physically abused have a very difficult time trusting anybody. Being very patient, calm, and caring will help one not to feel threatened. Using caution toward movements of the arm and hand or quick movements of the body must be stressed.

Jim was physically and mentally abused. Raising my arm caused him terror. I gave him eye contact, spoke in a soft voice, and let him know through my verbal and non-verbal actions that I was there to help not harm. After a while, he trusted me and slowly began progressing.

When I was a resource teacher in a small town, one young child, Dennis, who was the victim of physical and sexual abuse had a difficult time trusting others. Because of his fears of people and situations, he behaved negatively toward new people and new situations. After several months of intensive one-to-one time, he began to trust me. Through that trust, I was able to guide him to develop appropriate behaviors in the majority of situations. Slowly, he began developing behaviorally as well as cognitively.

In home situations, hugs are extremely important elements in letting one know that everything is okay. In school and clinical settings, hugs are no longer permitted because of sexual connotations. In those situations, a smile, a soft voice, and a pat on the hand or back indicate that you will guide them through the difficult times. Showing genuine caring of a person's needs, wants, and concerns helps in improvement and development of all areas. By observing the people I worked with and by responding to their reactions, I established a good working foundation. When they showed tenseness by clinching their fists, tightening their muscles, tapping on the desk, and crossing their arms, I then reevaluated the approach I used.

I used eye contact. I would explain the lessons or activities in a clear, concise manner. I would begin each lesson at a step they could understand and then proceeded from there. I would continually ask questions after presenting each step. I ensured that the environment was peaceful and not threatening. I played soft, quiet music which relaxed the body as well as the mind.

When I made home visits to young children who had deafness, blindness, or multiple disabilities and found their home environment in disarray, I would take the child to a peaceful, uncluttered environment. We went outside or to an area in the house that was not cluttered. The child then became more at ease and was able to attend to the lessons.

Being a good listener or good observer of body language is extremely important with all ages. With the babies with disabilities, I spent time reacting to their movements, sounds, and facial expressions. I responded with smiles and spoke to them about what they were doing. When they moved their arms or legs, I would gently touch that area and interpret what I believed they were trying to communicate. When they would make a sound, I would smile, point to their mouths, and then to my ears acknowledging that I heard them, showing them that listening to what they were trying to communicate was very important to me. With the older people who could communicate, I would ask pertinent questions about their feelings and their activities. With the nonverbal people of all ages, I interpreted their physical reactions or sounds to the material or the objects presented to them. I would then react accordingly. Facial expressions and body language can demonstrate a person's wants and needs more so than words can.

One adolescent, Sherri, had deafness, physical disabilities, and also had mental retardation. She began progressing in all areas when I began reading her body language and watching her facial expressions. I listened to the various pitches of sounds she was producing. This child used aggression to make her needs known. When I began interpreting what she was attempting to communicate, I was able to address each one of her needs and wants. She then began improving in all areas. This initiated the beginning of the "I Can" attitude.

A type of behavior modification program which was first initiated by B.F. Skinner assists in modifying behaviors. The basic premise of this program involves giving positive reinforcement for acceptable behavior and negative reinforcement for noncompliant behavior. Positive reinforcements should include smiles, pats on the backs, earning smiley faces, points, or tokens to be traded in for activities of interest or small enjoyable objects or food. Negative reinforcements include such things as time-out chairs and taking away of privileges, objects, and giving sad faces. An explanation of why a certain response was used is essential. Both the children and adults I worked with in institutions or schools responded favorably to this program.

Once the behavior was modified, I phased away from concrete reinforcements. I continued with the use of verbal reinforcements. This concept is often misunderstood because of the thought that behaviors should not be continually rewarded. But in everyday living, people are rewarded with money when one does a job or receive verbal reinforcement from others when one works and completes a job or task. Without reinforcements through money or without recognition, the "average" person will usually not perform or not work to their capability.

Role-playing the problem is a technique which brings the behavior to the forefront and brings a positive and understandable solution. This method is concrete, allowing the person to visualize the behavior and the solution. Using this technique, I role-played the person with disabilities and they role-played the part of the recipient of their negative behavior. After role-playing, we have an open discussion about how the negative behavior affected them and others. They discovered appropriate behaviors to replace the inappropriate ones. Jotting down the pros and cons of each behavior aided in visualizing the behaviors and deciding which reaction would be beneficial for all concerned.

In a work program, the people with disabilities are protected under the Americans with Disabilities Act.[3] This law protects people

---

[3] Arizona Center for Disability Law. *An Overview of the Employment Protection of Americans with Disability Act,* 10/01/01 p.7.

with disabilities from being discriminated against in everyday activities. Logical answers to the questions about the disability will help the other workers accept the person. Adapting work instructions to meet the cognitive needs will assist in preventing negative behaviors. The work supervisor should monitor the person with disabilities until a comfort zone has been established with all the workers. If at all possible, allow the person to learn the job at his own pace. This will help develop the "I Can" attitude.

This attitude will alleviate continuous problems both cognitively and behaviorally. By understanding various learning traits or behaviors, people will be able to recognize that people with disabilities can comfortably be integrated into most areas of society. However, the physical attributes need to be considered in applying for a specific job. For example a petite woman, whether there are signs of disabilities or not, should not apply for a job that requires heavy lifting of boards or construction material.

Another example was supplied to me by my sister, Linda Hoernke. She was a supervisor for the loading dock at the Milwaukee Post Office. A woman who is hearing impaired was hired. This woman could not hear the various trucks or forklifts. This could have been a dangerous situation for both the deaf person and the other workers. The post office also needed to hire an extra person to notify this woman of calls or of any potential dangers. This situation was not a constructive work environment for the woman. This situation also put a strain on the other workers and slowed down the progress of mail delivery.

Creating a relaxing, calming, and peaceful environment to work in or study in brings about a more peaceful attitude in dealing with various elements of work, school, or even home. While teaching or working in my home, I played peaceful music with nature sounds and soft instrumental sounds. This tends to relax the mind as well as the body. My students at first protested this music but as the lessons proceeded, they began picking the music they wanted to hear for the day. Even playing soft music in meetings changed the demeanor of the situation from stringent to a more relaxed one.

Discussions with the guardians and others involved in designing a consistent behavioral plan are a key element in dealing with and eliminating a behavioral problem. Using the same behavior plan in all elements of life is the key to success. Regardless of the behavioral technique implemented, consistency and the use of the "I Can" attitude are the key factors in modifying the behavior and allowing the person with disabilities to become a contributing member of our society.

Difficulties in the social realm can stem from a variety of behavioral problems. These are being shy, hostile, consistently challenging authority, throwing temper tantrums, being unwilling to comply with rules, dislike of social situations, rudeness, difficulty in interactions, evading responsibility, tending to lie, violating social codes, and doing many things at the spur of the moment. This person is usually the subject of teasing and jokes.

The essential components for the social realm are self-control in all social situations, human development including sex education, along with family orientation, age and gender identity, and teaching of mores and accepted rules of the society the person interacts with.

The foundations of the social realm are the use of proper conversations reflecting the differences between people and ages, observing privacy, awareness of modesty, ability to accept responsibility of actions and behaviors, and obtaining acceptable values. Modeling appropriate social skills is one of the better approaches to use. People learn social skills and characteristics by observing and then modeling. This is a definite factor in the acquired social skills of the people who are institutionalized. Observation and then modeling the behavior of different clients and staff produces many diverse social skills. This is the cause of confusion in setting a solid foundation for acceptable social skills. The social skills that are mimicked are ones which receive the most attention regardless of whether the skills were met with positive or negative consequences.

Teaching and modeling proper conversational skills are tremendously important in relating to people. Language is one area in life that is often a target for cruel jokes or mimicking. Whether there is a person with disabilities or a foreigner with an accent, they may face a series of rude comments, mimicking, or remarks. Since I have a speech impediment and speak at a slow pace, I was a target for insensitive people. When my speech became a subject for jokes, I would become flustered. This caused me to not speak correctly or not to speak at all. I observed this behavior in many of the people I worked with.

Because of being a target for verbal abuse, some refused to speak or express their thoughts. Taking the time to listen and respond to what is being said will help the person express himself. Encouragement to express one is a key component in building self-esteem. Showing interest in what someone says will make them feel important and not feel as if they are an outcast.

Since there is no censor of words used in movies or TV, some people tend to mimic what is heard. I have heard people of all ages swear proficiently but have a difficult time expressing themselves. Emphasis on acceptable and unacceptable language is extremely important. Reinforce language which is suitable for the situation. Consistency is a vital element for one learning appropriate speech and the context.

The teaching and modeling of correct language and syntax used in different arenas are vital. Dependent upon the intellectual level of the person, joining speaking clubs such as Toastmaster would be advantageous. If there is not a speaking club, which is related to the skills and communication level of a particular group, begin one. Being able to express oneself appropriately regardless of the type of interaction or situation is the beginning step to interacting socially.

Allowing a specific period for private time is imperative regardless if one is at home, in a clinic, or in a classroom setting. At this time, encourage looking at books, drawing, writing, or just thinking. Stress the importance of enjoying and making use of private time. Along with this, teach about respecting others' private time.

Another factor that deals with privacy is respecting ownership. Emphasize the concept of yours and mine. Stress asking permission before taking another's possession. Many children, even some adults, develop an attitude that if they want something, they take it. The idea of yours and mine should be taught at an early age and reinforced at all ages.

Modesty is another skill that should be approached at an early age. Society has somewhat accepted the fact that if a person has disabilities, especially mental retardation, modesty is not an important factor to teach. That is far from the truth. Modesty can be a learned skill with modeling, consistency, and practice. On an outing to a shopping mall with a group of adolescents with mental retardation, one male pulled down his pants and begin masturbating. I immediately directed him to the male bathroom. Afterwards, I had a long discussion with the group about appropriate places and times for different activities. By not getting angry but explaining in a quiet voice, he and others then learned the appropriate social requirements.

In our society, there are many people who refuse to accept responsibility for their actions or behaviors. Lying to cover up one's mistakes or behaviors is thought to be unacceptable but is a current practice in our society. People with disabilities watch the average person lie to get out of a situation then become confused when they are reprimanded. The process of questioning, patiently waiting and expecting truthful answers will assist in bringing out the truth.

In training one about values, the following areas must be taught. One must be consistent with messages, act upon values that are important, respect individual differences, and be able to discuss different values. Stress the fact that people are judged by not only what they do but also by what they say.

One young deaf boy, Mike, had no communication skills but he was taught values along with respecting other people's values from his father and mother at an early age. Despite having a limited vocabulary, his father was very cautious about modeling appropriate values. The son and father went to many social situations together. At an early age, the child became aware of respecting himself and others. This child learned honesty, appropriate interaction with people of all ages, and developed a good set of values. These behaviors were stepping stones for the boy to function appropriately in society. Once this child learned communication, he began to progress quickly in all areas—social, cognitive, behavioral, and emotional.

On the other side, children and adults with disabilities who live in dysfunctional homes or institutions have no consistent role models. They become stagnant in their abilities to socialize and to even progress in all areas of life. They truly lack an appropriate set of values. Values need to be demonstrated consistently throughout the day both in the learning and home environments.

One mother brought her four-year-old, Sue, to my house for special tutoring. While the mother and I were talking, Sue ventured out to my front yard, pulled down her pants, and proceeded to go to the bathroom. This behavior was frequently done at home.

When I saw this, I took Sue by the hand and showed her what she did. I then shook my head and made a disgusting look on my face and said no. I took her to the bathroom, pointed to the toilet, and moved my head up and down. I placed Sue upon the toilet and gave her verbal reinforcement. I then created a plan to teach the child, along with her mother, values of respecting oneself. Appropriate values need to be demonstrated consistently throughout the day in one's life.

Identity and sexuality are extremely important issues to be taught. Many people are embarrassed to discuss this, especially with their children. Identity of the body must begin once a child discovers different areas of their body. Proper identification of body parts should be expressed in proper terms. Using "baby language" and then changing to appropriate language as one matures is confusing. As the child grows, pointing out different parts on dolls or pictures and then comparing with the actual body part will help the child in establishing his/her identity. Being familiar with good or bad touches in specific areas will assist in alleviating some sexual advances.

From 1978 to 1980, I taught a sex education class, with the help of Planned Parenthood, to adolescents in an institution. These adolescents had been either institutionalized most of their lives, lived in group homes, or had very protected home lives. Because of this, the majority were unaware of the differences between female and male bodies and unaware of their identities. This caused problems interacting with society.

One mentally handicapped adolescent, Victor, loved hugging and kissing anybody he had just met. By teaching him appropriate touching, self-identity, and identity of male and female, he was then able to interact properly in society.

Many people have the false impression that if a person has emotional, mental, or physical disabilities, he does not have emotional or physical feelings. This is far from the truth. All human beings are equipped with physical, emotional, and even sexual feelings. When asking permission to teach the sex education class, many of the guardians were stunned. After explaining the need for the child to learn, they reluctantly gave permission. By being aware of all the social implications in our culture, the people I taught were able to deal with many social situations. We discussed the mental and physical differences of males and females, interaction with both sexes, dating, marriage, and the responsibility along with pros and cons of having children. Discussions on human awareness are extremely important, as then the special person will become aware of his and others' sexuality. Being more aware will prevent the person with disabilities from being taken advantage of.

Emotional factors vary in degree of severity. The emotional factors consist of fear, rage, depression, hostility, unusual sleep patterns, thoughts of suicide, and the "don't care" attitude. Emotional problems within the educational systems are observed as follows:

a) The inability to learn which cannot be explained by intellectual, sensory, or health factors.

b) An inability to acquire or maintain satisfactory interpersonal relationships.

c) Inappropriate types of behavior or feelings under normal circumstances.

d) A development of physical symptoms due to fears associated with situations or activities connected with personal problems.

e) Continuous depressed moods or unhappiness.

f) Insensitivity to others. Problems in these areas need to be coordinated with a mental health professional: counselor, psychologist, or psychiatrist.

Watching the person with disabilities' body language is the first step in detecting an emotional outburst toward an activity or circumstance. Dealing with the problem in the very early stages will prevent the problem from escalating. Encouraging writing thoughts in a journal and then discussing the pros and cons of each feeling will help in finding an appropriate way to solving the problem before it escalates. With younger children or people who have mental retardation, present a chart divided into time increments. During each increment, draw smiley or sad faces indicating the behavior or emotion of that period of time. Throughout the day, discuss the incidences behind the sad or happy faces. As their target behavior or skill improves and is replaced with appropriate ones, slowly phase away from the drawing of the faces. Self-satisfaction that a problem can be solved peacefully becomes the major reinforcement.

All people are more optimistic about themselves when they are approached with a positive attitude. One gentleman I worked with in a mental institution had a very difficult time interacting with people. By my being interested in what he had to say, we established a rapport. Regardless of the age or disability, a person will respond and progress if a feeling of comfort is established.

There are various degrees of comfort for each individual. To determine a person's comfort zone, take time to listen and watch the body language. Many people tend to produce mixed messages such as verbalizing in a positive manner but exhibiting negative body language. This occurs not only with people with disabilities; I have observed mixed messages with some professionals. Through these mixed messages, the person with disabilities becomes confused on what to expect. Because of this, some may even respond with hostile characteristics.

When dealing with a potential problem, it is of extreme importance to keep calm and collected. Be aware of not speaking more loudly than usual. I have observed persons with disabilities control the situation, therefore controlling the people involved. At times, they perform certain mannerisms that knowingly will set off other people. Not reacting to their emotional outbursts will help in minimizing or eradicating the problem. Striving to maintain conversations and activities on a positive basis will elicit a more reliable and predictable response.

The physically impaired have a loss in the areas of movement or function. Either gross motor (the large muscles) or fine motor (the movement of muscles like in the fingers) could be affected.

Physical disability varies in each individual in the type and severity. Many people associate the person with physical disabilities with an array of other disabilities, particularly mental retardation. Despite the areas affected, the person with physical disabilities can succeed by adapting the right equipment and programs to the physical needs of that individual. Promoting the "I Can" attitude toward progressing and achieving goals can be a major influence toward achieving independence in many areas of life.

One child with physically disabilities, Bonnie, had no movement of her arms or legs. She could not speak. Her head was the only area of her body she could move and control. I connected a pointer to a head band. Developing and then training Bonnie in the use of a communication chart which was mounted on cardboard, she eventually was able to communicate her wants and needs. Using pictures in the communication chart of areas and objects which were in her immediate environment, she was able to communicate by pointing. Through this method, she developed the "I Can" attitude toward progressing and achieving. Bonnie began succeeding in many areas of her life. Her mom was overwhelmed when Bonnie pointed to the words and pictures "I Love You."

Regardless of the disability, a person using the "I Can" attitude will ensure success in many areas. Having a positive attitude despite physical or mental disadvantages can change a person's disadvantages to advantages.

Each of the following chapters will be dedicated to a specific disability. Throughout these chapters, I will show that with love, patience, and foremost the "I Can" attitude that remarkable changes can occur in achieving goals, wants, and needs in the public, school, and home environments.

ADDITIONAL REFERENCES

Organizations

American Disability Association
2201 6th Ave.
Birmingham, Alabama

Phone 205-251-7417
Fax 205-328-9090
Email www.ada.org

Council for Exceptional Children
1110 North Globe Rd. Suite 300
Arlington, Virginia 22201

Phone 703-602-3660
Fax 703-264-9494
TTY 866-915-5000

Disabled People International
748 Broadway
Winnipeg, Manitoba, Canada

Phone 204-287-8010
Fax 204-783-6270
E-mail info@dpi.org

Easter Seal Society
230 W. Monroe St., Suite 1800
Chicago, Illinois 60606

Phone 312-726-6200
TTY 312-726-4258
Fax 312-726-1494

Inclusion Network
312 Walnut St. Suite 1160
Cincinnati, Ohio 45202

Phone 513-345-1330
TTY 513-345-1336
Fax 513-345-1337

World Associations of Persons
With Disability
4503 Sunnyview Dr. Suite 1121
P.O. Box 1411
Oklahoma City, Oklahoma 73135

Phone 405-672-4440
Fax 405-672-4441

National Organization on Disability
910 16 St., NW
Washington DC 20006

E-Mail:www.nod.org

PERIODICALS AND NEWSLETTERS

ABDC News-   Phone 800-313-ABDC

Association of Birth Defect   Email:
Children   abdc@ birth defects.org
827 Irma Avenue
Orlando, California 32803

Access to Travel
ACCESS to Travel/SATH
PO Box 352 Hawley Lane
New Baltimore, New York
12124

Exceptional Parent   Fax 201-634-6599
555 Kinderkamack Road   Phone 201-634-6550
Oradell, NJ 07649

PALAESTRA-   Phone 309-833-1902
PO Box 508
Macomb, IL 61455

Ability Magazine   Phone 714-854-8700
P.O. Box 10655
Costa Mesa, California 92627

Active Living   Phone 905-6016
2276 Rosedene Rd.
St. Ann's ON LOR 1 yo,
Canada

Careers & the disABLED   Phone 516-9421
1160 E. Jericho Tpke, Suite
200
Huntington, New York 11743

BOOKS

Living with a Disability	Howard Rusk
No Apologies: A Guide to Living With a Disability	Florence Weiner
Missing Pieces: A Chronicle of Living With a Disability	Kenneth Irving
Getting It: Persuading Organizations And Individuals to Be More Comfortable With People with Disabilities	Melissa Marshall
You Will Dream New Dreams	Stanley D. Klein, PHD Kim Schute
Living With a Brother or Sister with Special Needs: A Book for Sibs	Donald J. Meyer
People With Disabilities	Cory Silverburg
A Special Raccoon: Helping A Child Learn About Handicaps	S. Brent, MD

Chapter II

CHALLENGES OF MENTAL RETARDATION

The major detriment to the advancement of people with mental retardation is people's preconceived attitudes and false perceptions of what a person with mental retardation can or cannot do. Regardless of their mental or physical capabilities, they can achieve many tasks if compassion, patience, and the "I Can" attitude are supplied. These people do have the emotional aptitude for feelings. The ones who may not be able to verbally express their wants and needs can communicate their thoughts through facial expressions and body language. Regardless of the IQ, a person with mental retardation can detect if a person is relating to them or is a detriment to their success.

This was often the case working in an institution for mental retardation. These people attempted to achieve tasks that were presented by the staff that were responsive to their needs. On the other hand, they refused to attend to any task when a staff member was not understanding and helpful toward them.

During shower time, one staff member refused to help or aid a preteen, Sue, with a shower. Sue became very frustrated which developed into behavioral problems. I intervened, reinforced and guided her when she needed help. She eventually proceeded to do this task independently.

The main basis of interactions with mental retardation is to remember that they are people, too, equipped with feelings, emotions, and the want to achieve. If people with mental retardation are treated with respect, patience, compassion, and understanding, they will be able to achieve many tasks that were previously thought to be impossible.

People diagnosed with mental retardation have a limited intellectual level and have limitations in two or more adaptive skills which include communication, home living, self-care, social skills, community use, health and safety, leisure, academics, and work. Mental retardation begins before one is eighteen years old. It is detected by a score of seventy or lower on a standardized IQ test.

Factors that can cause mental retardation are biomedical, social, behavioral, and educational. These are interrelated during the life of the individual.[4]

Biomedical refers to the biological development of the person. Genetics and nutrition play an important role in this area. One family, to whom I made home visits, did not supply their infant,

---

[4] American Association for Mental Retardation. *Mental Retardation Fact Sheet.* 1/12004, p. 6 of 7.

Carol, who had mental retardation with the proper nutrition. Because of the lack of proper nutrition for development, the child did not develop mentally or physically. After teaching the mother proper nutrition, the child began to show marked improvements mentally and physically.

The social realm includes interactions with families or society. Children whose guardians were not ashamed of them progressed in all developmental areas. These children developed appropriately in the area of social skills as well as communication and self-help skills. As adults, most were able to live either in a semi-independent or totally independent living situation. The children who were institutionalized and had no or very little home structure became totally dependent upon society as an adult.

One young adolescent, Mary, I began working with in the institution was afraid of socializing or interacting with anyone. Mary was brought up as an outcast in her home environment. Because of the mental retardation, she was taught no skills. Her parents believed she was a bad omen from God. She had to survive with very little developmental awareness. Because of this, she was afraid of everything and everyone. Mary's communication skills consisted of pointing, yelling, grunts, and using facial expressions along with body language. After one-to-one training, she began to trust me. I established a relationship with her through patience, love, compassion, and instilling the "I Can" attitude. Once that trust was established, she developed socially, behaviorally, and academically. She began communicating using sign language and speech. I eventually faded away from the sign language.

Behavioral factors are developed at a very early age. If the child is taught that there is a consequence for negative behavior and reinforcement for positive behavior, then the child will be conditioned to exhibit appropriate behaviors. Consistently giving positive reinforcement for good behaviors and negative reinforcement for bad behaviors establishes a sound foundation for acceptable manners. With the person who has mental retardation, a very concrete approach is fundamental in teaching and then being able to retain which behaviors are acceptable.

There are many types of behavior which indicate mental retardation. They often forget or have poor memory skills. They have difficulty in following through on tasks. Their attention span is short. Compared to their peers, they act younger than their age and rely too much on other people for directions and guidance. If people with mental retardation do not understand situations or concepts and are not redirected, they may become disruptive or retreat into a world of their own. This is indicative of the children with mental retardation who were incarcerated at detention centers. Since they were not shown attention, given guidance and redirection, or made to feel that they played an important role in their living environments, they began to comply with the wishes of gang members. The gang members provided the people with mental retardation with much needed attention. Therefore, they became a patsy for crimes committed.

John, a fourteen-year-old boy with mental retardation, shot and killed a person. The gang enticed him to perform this terrible deed. He had received acceptance from the gang members because they gave him a false feeling of being accepted and liked. He did not realize the consequences of his actions until after his court hearing. He was committed to the adolescent section in an adult prison. After the court hearing, John came into my classroom with tears streaming down his face trying to make sense of the direction which his life had taken. If anybody had come into contact with John and provided him with positive reinforcements toward good behavior, his self-worth would have been much better. He more than likely would have a better perspective of himself and his life. It takes all of society, not only guardians and teachers, to assist in the development of a person, especially if that person has mental, emotional, and/or physical problems.

On the positive side, the people with mental retardation usually enjoy the simple things in life and accept happenings and people as they are. When I went on walks with groups of people with mental retardation in the mountains or the desert, they taught me to appreciate and love the basic things in life. They showed appreciation and excitement over flowers along a roadside, the beauty of the sky and land, and the beauty within each individual. They enjoyed these moments as this was a time to relax and connect to nature. At these times, they were not worried about other people's perceptions of them. They enjoyed the time to be themselves without restrictions or false expectations.

The educational factors are based upon early involvement and interactions within the family and society in promoting adaptive skills and mental development. Through testing and observations, professionals have become conscious that to ensure learning and retention of skills, early intervention is vital. Once the child is school age, their progress is reliant upon many factors. Most important is the guardians' attitude toward education and definitely toward the child's mental and physical capabilities. The responsibility of the community, guardians, and school to work as a team in meeting the needs of the child is imperative.

The stimulation and response from the adults in the family and in society have an impact upon the development of the child and the progression into adulthood. This is reflective of times I went into the homes of children with mental retardation. The homes which provided a nurturing, caring environment facilitated the person with mental retardation to succeed in many areas regardless of the functioning capability of the child. These homes had picture books and designated story times throughout the day. To discover the importance of words, the printed word of a specific object was placed on the object. This approach is the first step in learning about letters and words. Comparing the word recognized to the same word in a book can be the initial step in reading.

The homes which provided the bare necessities for survival of the child weakened the child's psychological, physical, mental, and social developments. If there is not a strong support system in schools, homes, and in public, the mentally disabled person will be targeted for failure.

One baby, Sally, was a victim of the mother's substance abuse and neglect. Sally was not stimulated mentally or physically. She was not taught proper self-help skills, communication skills, or adaptive behaviors. This child did not begin functioning until she had home-intervention programs. With the lack of follow-through in home-based programs, therapy programs, and lack of parental supervision, Sally was eventually taken out of the home situation. Upon being placed in a stimulating home environment where she received love, patience, kindness, and positive guidance, she began progressing in all areas. Through this positive home intervention, Sally was shown the "I Can" attitude toward all activities that were presented to her. She was shown that she was an okay person and that she was an important person to many people. The "I Can" attitude and feelings of acceptance made a major impact upon Sally. She began responding optimistically to all tasks and interactions, therefore increasing her knowledge in academics and all adaptive skills.

Many times, when a person is labeled with a specific disability, certain characteristics are placed upon that person. Once a person has the label of mental retardation, they are not expected to achieve further than what the label dictates. This is a very common misperception among people in their response to people with mental retardation. I had often exposed the person with mental retardation to events or happenings in public.

One time, I took several adolescents with mental retardation to a shopping center. As we exited from the state van and began walking toward the mall, we were stared at by a mother with her five-year-old son. The mother grabbed her son and said in a loud voice, "Stay away from them. They may hurt you." That really hurt the feelings of each of the adolescents I was with. They felt they were being persecuted for no reason. Understanding the importance for me to speak to this lady, the adolescents with mental retardation voluntarily sat down on benches while one of the boys and I walked over to the woman and her child. I spoke to her in a very calm voice explaining that there was no reason for her to be scared. I explained that this group was similar to the majority of people except for their slower thought processes and slower physical movements. We invited her and her son to have ice tea at a restaurant with us. Hesitantly, she conceded. By talking to each one of the adolescents, she discovered that they were not anything to be afraid of or to mock. She thanked each one for changing her negative perception of mental retardation.

Through this experience and ones similar to it, the adolescents with mental retardation were challenged to deal with a variety of reactions from a wide mixture of people. Many people would remark that since they have the label of mental retardation, they cannot perform certain activities nor do specific tasks. With the "I Can" attitude, these special people have surprised the person with no disabilities by their expression of appropriate emotions or by accomplishing many tasks that were thought impossible.

On many other occasions in public, both adults and children with no disability would point or imitate the way of talking, walking, or behaving. These inconsiderate reactions would destroy the self-esteem of people with mental retardation. I spent many hours consoling and reminding them that they are okay people. Educating and encouraging people to be conscientious about the impact of their reactions toward people with mental retardation will increase the overall understanding and knowledge of the general treatment of these special people. These people need to be treated with the kind of respect that is given to any other person.

Working in an institution for people with mental retardation, two other staff members, Karen Johnson and Randy Smith, and I planned a trip to Disneyland and the beach with ten of the clients. When I first approached the director of the institution, I was told that funds were not readily available for a trip such as that, but if I found the funds, we could go. That obstacle did not stop us. We decided to provide the children with the responsibility of raising the money.

Karen, Randy, and I collaborated and decided which adolescents we were going to take on the trip. A few of the people we picked were perceived as questionable candidates for this trip due to their behavioral problems. Because of placing responsibility on them and treating them as a person without a disability, they all acted appropriately before, during, and even after the trip. Having confidence placed upon them promoted positive self-esteem and the desire to be a responsible person.

When asking permission from the legal guardians, many of them responded with shock. They had a very difficult time assessing why we would want to take their institutionalized child with mental retardation on a trip of this magnitude. Many of the guardians questioned their lack of ability to raise money and be responsible on this trip. However, after much persuasion, all of them did give permission. Many of the guardians remarked after we returned from the trip that their attitudes toward what their child could achieve had totally changed.

For lodging, I called March Air Force Base and the commander gave us lodging at the Bachelor Officers' Quarters for a minimum price. The state provided us with a state van and even a state credit card for gas. Money was still a major factor for going on this trip.

After speaking with managers of many grocery stores in Tucson, Arizona about having bake sales, they all gave their authorization. Baking and selling of the baked goods provided lessons in work ethics. Randy, Karen, and I would spend nights and weekends supervising the chosen adolescents in preparing and then selling baked goods outside of local stores. We raised several thousand dollars. Through this experience, the children grasped many of the concepts in adaptive skills. These adolescents learned planning skills, money concepts and management, communication skills, self-direction, skills in baking and then selling of the baked goods, the ability to interact appropriately with many different people in public, responsibility, and following directions and rules. They even learned some math, reading, and writing skills in following the directions in cookbooks, and in making posters to advertise our bake sales and collecting money for the baked goods.

This trip also promoted learning of practical skills such as preparing for the trip in deciding on what clothes, personal items, and how much money to bring. We also taught basic map reading. With assistance, they helped plot out the trip on the map. Even though we would distribute their medications, these adolescents with mental retardation learned which medications were needed and at what time the medications needed to be distributed. We made small paper clocks with the time their medication was distributed. They compared their clocks to the wall clocks. Plus teaching time, this gave them the responsibility for reminding us that it was time for medications.

Prior to the trip, we discussed and then role-played proper behaviors and manners used in restaurants and other public places. Through this, they learned acceptable behaviors and skills while interacting with the public. In a restaurant one night, the only "problem" was that one of the boys, Bob, picked up his plate when he finished his meal. He then began heading to the kitchen to wash it. This was a common necessary behavior in the institution. We spent time explaining that one of the paid jobs in a restaurant was to take the dirty plates to the kitchen and another person would wash the dirty plates. The children were totally amazed that a strange person would be responsible for cleaning up after they had eaten.

Disneyland was a totally new and wondrous experience for both the teenagers and the staff. To see and enjoy Disneyland through the eyes of children with mental retardation made me realize what a fabulous, exciting place this was.

Each one of them was very excited about venturing out to the beach. Most of them had never seen a beach except on TV or the movies. We went to Kentucky Fried Chicken and picked up a "Family Meal" and soda. We spread out blankets and had a picnic on the beach. During the picnic, we reminisced about our adventure to Disneyland. We also talked about the many wondrous things we were seeing at the beach. After lunch, we spent the time collecting seashells, wading into the ocean, and forming imaginary objects from the cloud formations. They began to share their feelings and excitement with each other. This opened the doors of communication. They developed connections to nature and to the others who were on this journey.

This trip was a dream of a lifetime. The majority of the children had spent the major part of their young lives in institutions or in homes that provided no love, attention, or acceptance. Once the adolescents were given responsibility and a dream of venturing to a place they had only seen on TV, they all behaved extraordinarily well. When the expectations were placed upon them, these children responded appropriately. The highlight of the trip for one Down's syndrome child, Dustin, was to meet Mickey Mouse at Disneyland. For many years after, he would point to Mickey Mouse on TV and tell everyone he met the famous mouse. Even several years after this trip, I would run into these people in public and all they talked about was the trip to Disneyland and to the beach. It is amazing to realize how much they remembered and learned from this adventure.

This definitely indicates that a person can retain information if it is presented in a way that has meaning to one's life. Once these children with mental retardation realized that they could achieve what was considered impossible, they began progressing in many other areas. This trip changed their attitudes from "I can't" to "I Can."

Regardless of the intellectual level of a person, when given a concrete set of plans along with the awareness that they can learn, there will be a definite gain in self-esteem. This will promote one to achieve. Success is inevitable. What was once thought of as impossible can become reality by using the "I Can" approach.

Both children and adults with whom I worked improved when provided with sequential short-term goals in order to reach their long-term goals. I would spend time explaining each step along the way in clear, precise language. I was careful to only speak in simple sentences and encouraged each one to ask questions as soon as a doubt arose. To ensure success, there needed to be a complete understanding of the step being focused upon before continuing to the next step. Continuous repetition of each learned step is essential. Using all five senses in the process of learning is an essential step for retaining the material. With assistance in reading or spelling, I wrote words in blue magic marker on sandpaper and then had the person verbalize while tracing over each letter. In color therapy, the color blue relates to the brain. Another method is to place an index card underneath the sentence being read. This helps with focusing on a particular word or group of words. Sign language, the Signing Exact English approach, and speech promotes learning of spelling and reading of individual words. I used this method with a twelve-year-old, Ray, who could not read. He eventually learned to read. This energized Ray to work on other academics that were once an unattainable mystery to him.

When a person had difficulty in the phonetic approach to reading, I would match pictures with the nouns in the passages. I then would have them trace the word on sandpaper, say the word out loud, and match the picture to the word. After much repetition, I phased away from the pictures. Reading became a learned skill. They eventually learned the connecting words (and, so, because, etc.) by finger-spelling or tracing on sandpaper.

The concepts of the Support Program developed by the American Association for Mental Retardation about fifteen years ago promote individualism. This is defined "as the resources and individual strategies necessary to promote the development, education, interest, and personal well-being of a person with mental retardation."[5] There are nine areas in which the person needs support and training. These activities are as follows: Human Development, Training and Education, Home Living, Community Living, Employment, Health and Safety, Behavioral, Social, and Protection and Advocacy.[6] Each specific area includes facets of living that when learned, will support the person who has retardation to individually function in society to the best of his capabilities. The training is initiated by any appropriate person or agency which is in direct contact with the person who has a mental disability. Individualizing each program promotes true understanding and well-being for the individual. The Support Program is a step toward inclusion into society and better acceptance and awareness of the ones who have mental

---

[5] American Association on Mental Retardation. *Fact Sheet.* 1/01/04, p. 4 of 7.

[6] American Associations on Mental Retardation. *Fact Sheet.* 1/01/04, p. 4-5 of 7.

retardation. The "I Can" attitude and positive reinforcements can promote success in all areas of the Support Program.

In schools, a child with mental retardation is a usual target for cruel and unprecedented jokes and remarks. When the other students are trained to accept each individual and assist, instead of mocking students who apparently need help, then that student as well as the student with mental disabilities will grow psychologically, behaviorally, socially, and even academically.

Presently, most educational systems believe in inclusion. Because of this concept, many of the children with mental retardation are placed in a regular classroom with the help of a specialized teacher or assistant for a period of time. The success of the person with intellectual disabilities is dependent upon parents, teachers, specialists, therapists, counselors, medical staff, his peers in school, the community, and the motivation and perseverance of the person with mental retardation. Having people who have mental retardation be a part of the classroom activities will encourage self-determination plus be a positive mode in learning to interact with peers. Having a reliable peer tutor in class will help with feelings of acceptance.

The task of finding an appropriate job involves taking into account the factors of the mentality and the physical capability of the job seeker. Skills and thorough study in finding a job through the newspaper, employment offices, or employment areas in stores is essential. The study of work ethics and the responsibility of a job are essential. This includes inappropriate and appropriate conversations and behaviors while at work, appropriate time for arriving and leaving work, and the responsibility for accomplishing work as to the best of one's capability. A very important factor is encouraging and instilling the concept that asking for help when in doubt is okay. Counseling and discussions about reactions the people with mental retardation receive from coworkers is extremely important.

Knowledge of basic skills in interacting and surviving in society are essential. This is applicable to all ages. Included in this are the following skills: reading public signs, being aware of traffic lights in so far as crossing the street, money concepts, job skills, public transportation, socializing in and outside of the family, basic reading skills, and learning responsibility in being a productive member of society. Awareness of public resources and interactions with the public is a crucial skill to be taught.

The study of public transportation will ensure people with retardation independence. Teaching of bus routes and basic time and money concepts will prepare them for the experience of public bus transportation. In the beginning, guide the people with mental retardation through all facets of riding the bus. Slowly phase away guidance as the person can show independence. Having the time of bus arrival and departure on a clock made from index cards will help with retention. Speaking to the bus drivers to encourage and guide successful completion of the bus ride will ensure victory. When the first successful trip is made independently, over-reinforce this accomplishment.

Demonstrations and teaching of proper conversational techniques will aid in the acceptance and independence of the people with mental retardation in public. Many of the people with mental retardation I worked with had a difficult time in distinguishing between what was appropriate or inappropriate conversation to specific groups of people. Role-playing, meetings, and conversations with various groups of people will help. Consistent reminders and modeling of correct behaviors and conversations will be helpful.

When speaking to a mentally challenged person, take the time to really listen to them. Giving eye contact is very important. This is a way of determining their unspoken communication through body language. When I don't understand them, I question the meaning of what they are trying to express. Upon meeting a person with mental retardation, taking the time to respond in a positive manner will make a huge difference for that person.

My father, Robert Lorenzen, told me of one situation. My father was standing at a busy street corner waiting for the light to change. A woman standing next to him was approached by a man with mental retardation. This man told the woman that she was beautiful. Instead of being shocked and fearful, the woman thanked him. This one small friendly gesture made that man feel good. My father noted a smile on the person with mental retardation's face indicating that he was very pleased. Small actions like that can make a difference in anybody's life.

Appropriate touch is essential to teach. Some people with mental retardation enjoy hugging anyone who shows them attention. Stressing the importance of the handshake as opposed to the hug is extremely important. On an outing to a store, Victor, a young adolescent, became confused when he hugged a store clerk for helping him and the clerk responded negatively. After that incident, I continuously went over strategies for appropriate and acceptable behavior in public. Incidences such as this should also be dealt with in a sex education class or a human awareness class.

In teaching a sex education class, I taught appropriate touch and appropriate conversations to different groups of people. When discussing different body parts or different actions, I was extremely conscious of not speaking in "baby language." I used the proper terms. Expressing things in a child-like way would only confuse the person with mental retardation at times when the correct wordage was used. Also, using child-like terms in public would be a demonstration to other people of the person's mental disabilities.

Time spent in talking to people with mental retardation about some people's rude mannerisms or remarks toward them is vital. The realization that this will happen and teaching how to handle such situations are important. Stress that there are differences in all people. Point out that each individual person has their own special mannerisms. When they encounter rude people, they should walk away. Being upset over what one says is not worth it. After any unfortunate incident, it is of extreme importance to know that speaking to someone about the occurrence will assist in learning from the experience. Making time to express thoughts and feelings over a situation will help dissolve any pent-up anger.

Time, patience, and compassion toward the person with mental retardation are the building blocks toward instilling the "I Can" attitude.

ADDITIONAL REFERENCES

Organizations

American Association on Mental
Retardation
444 N. Capital St.
Washington D.C. 200011-1512

Phone 800-424-3668

ARC of the United States
1010 Wayne Ave., Suite 650
Silverspring, Maryland 20910

Phone 301-565-3842
Fax 301-565-3843

Best Buddies
100 SE 2nd St. #1990
Miami, Florida 33131

Phone 800-89 Buddy
Fax 305-374-2233

Citizens Care, Inc.
8 Haltman Dr.
Coroapolis, Pennsylvania 15108

Phone 412-771-0232

National Down Syndrome Society
666 Broadway
New York, New York 10012

Phone 800-221-979-2827
Fax 221-979-2827
Email www.ndss.org

President's Committee for People
With Intellectual Disabilities
Room 701 Aerospace Center
370 L'Enfant Promenade SW
Washington DC 20447

Phone 202-619-0634
Fax 202-205-9514
Email satwater@act.hhs.gov

PERIODICALS AND NEWSLETTERS

AAMR Newsletters

P.O. Box 1897

Lawrence, KS 66044-8897

1)*American Journal on Mental Retardation*

2)*AAMRFYI*—online newsletter.

3)*Mental Retard*ation.

Oppenheim Toy Portfolio

40 E. 9th Suite 14m

New York, NY 10003

Voting Rights of People with Mental Disorders

www.bazelon.org

Persons With Mental Disabilities

www.tcheose.state.tx.us

BOOKS

With a Little Help From My Friends

Presidents Committee for People with Intellectual Disabilities.

Aerospace Center

370 L'Enfant Promenade

Washington D.C. 20447

(5 booklets)

1) *Speaking Up Speaking Out*

2) *Growing Strong*

3) *Real Lives*

4) *I Am Who I Am*

5) *Choosing Systems*

Positive Behavior Support Training AAMR

Curriculum 2003 Special Issue

John Rush and Allen Frances, Editors

A Family-Centered Approach to People With Mental Retardation

Linda Leal, PhD

A Guide to Consent

Robert Dinerstein, J.D.,

Stanley Herr, J.D., D. Phil,

Joan O'Sullivan, J.D

A Family Handbook on Future Planning

ARC of the U.S.

Sharon Davis, Editor

Chapter III

FRUSTRATING WORLD OF LEARNING DISABILITIES

A learning disability is a condition which is not physically apparent. The deficit is in the inability to understand or process skills in one or more of the following academics: thinking, reading, spelling, math, and spoken or written language. The major difficulty is created by a disorder in processing language receptively or expressively. Problems in coordination can also be evident. Having trouble in attending or concentrating on the task at hand is prevalent. Difficulties in perceiving and understanding the actions of other people are widely apparent with this disability. One of the major setbacks can stem from the reaction of other people perceiving the learning disabilities as mental retardation. Unlike mental retardation, these people have average or above average intelligence. Learning disabilities are a lifelong challenge. Through training, a person can learn ways to compensate for their problems.

There have been debates on the actual causes of learning disabilities because there are a variety of possible causes. A major cause is activated by types of disturbances in various areas of the brain. The type of difficulty is dependent upon which area of the brain is affected. There are major differences between achievement and intellectual abilities. I have worked with both adults and children who are able to thrive in many areas but cannot accomplish various activities in one of the areas involving spoken or written language, listening comprehension, math reasoning, reading, or writing. One friend of mine, Steve, had no problems with speaking, comprehending, or remembering what others said. His only problem was spelling. He continually printed letters or words backwards. For example, he wrote "w" as "m," "p" as "q," or "bad" as "dab." He had a very difficult time writing reports. Deaf finger-spelling and tracing words on sandpaper aided him with his spelling. He began writing on light blue paper and/or with a blue pen as that helped in retention. Blue is the color which relates to the brain. He also took time to review what he had written and compared problem letters or words with words already written.

The brain stem is formed during the early stages of pregnancy. This controls basic functions such as breathing and digestion. The thinking area of the brain is developed and is divided into two halves. As new cells develop, they move into areas creating networks to share information between the areas.[7] If this development is interrupted, then disabilities will occur. Some professionals believe this is the beginning of learning disabilities or some type of learning disorder.

Injuries to the brain could occur during the birth process when there is rapid or difficult labor. Also, premature babies have a greater risk of developing learning disabilities. Pregnant women need to be cautious of eating correctly and of limiting certain strenuous activities. Substance abuse, drinking, smoking, or taking drugs are definitely detrimental to the welfare of the unborn baby. The beginning of a disability could be created by uncaring or unknowing parents. I have spoken to many parents who continue to use the debilitating substances despite the possibility of producing more children.

There have been studies on the belief that learning disabilities may be genetically linked. On the other hand, some professionals feel that the cause of a learning disability is environmental more so than genetics. In the majority of cases, the child from infancy into childhood will mimic the caregiver who is constantly in contact with the child. If the caregiver has learning disabilities and is the only consistent model, then the child may mimic some disorders. To prevent this from happening, there must be interventions from specialists or other family members. I observed this predicament many times at my jobs as a special education teacher and as a parent advisor.

---

[7] University Of Saskatchewan. *Who is Eligible: Learning Disabilities.* p. 7 of 24.

If an infant is exposed to toxins in the environment, the process in brain development may be disrupted.[8] This is another cause of learning disabilities or other types of disabilities. Lead or cadmium for steel products can be devastating agents. Cadmium, which is involved in the process of making steel products, can get into the soil which has a direct effect upon the food we eat.[9] Checking the possibility of environmental toxins in the area one lives is necessary, especially if a possibility exists of creating a new life. For workers in a copper-mining town, there was controversy on whether the environmental toxins had affected or created some challenged children.

The academic terms relating to learning disabilities are dyslexia, dysgraphia, dyscalculia, and attention deficit with or without hyperactivity. Dyslexia is having problems with reading. Dysgraphia is having difficulty with writing. Dyscalculia is having trouble with the mathematical process. With each one of these specific problems, incorporating as many senses as possible into the process of learning is very important. The use of manipulatives aids in retention. Repetition of learned concepts is essential. In progressing to a new step, I included the learned material in with the new material. I implemented the use of both the senses and repetition with all ages—infants through adults.

---

[8] University of Saskatchewan, op.cit., p.8 of 24.

[9] Ibid., p.8 of 24.

[9] *National Resources for Adults with Learning Disabilities.* Page 3, 3/19/2004.

Attention deficit is having problems concentrating on the task at hand. Attention deficit hyperactivity is when a person has a tendency to interrupt and talk constantly. This individual appears nervous, has difficulty sitting still, and cannot pay attention to one task too long.

Jody, a seven-year-old with attention deficit disorder, had a very difficult time sitting still for more than five minutes. By incorporating the use of her senses in the process of learning, she began paying attention for longer periods of time. She had her own cubicle in the classroom where she could not visually be distracted. She also had earphones connected to a small tape recorder. Soft and soothing music played. Using a behavior modification system of reinforcements for good behavior and attending to the task gave her motivation to pay attention and accomplish work. I created a chart with each hour of the school day divided up into five-minute increments. When she did well, I gave her a happy face to put in that increment. When she was not attending and hyper, I gave her a sad face for that increment. I showed a happy or sad face when I handed her the specific corresponding sticker. After she received five happy faces in a row, she received a fourth of a glass of her favorite juice. When she began succeeding by receiving happy faces for four increments, then I increased the amount of happy faces she needed to six. By continually extending the amount of faces for her award, she began attending to the task at hand with more frequency.

A person with learning disabilities may be hindered because of being unable to respond to body movements, facial expressions, or in having sensitivity to being touched. To overcome these disorders, it takes time, repetition, and patience.

When ten-year-old Bob was diagnosed as learning disabled and placed in my resource room, he had a difficult time emotionally and academically. After years of failing, he developed the attitude that he was dumb and could not learn anything.

Bob's lessons began with material on auditory and visual perceptions. The lessons began in discrimination of likeness or differences of sounds, letters, and numbers. First, we began with environmental sounds and then proceeded with speech sounds. Repeating sounds or words from prerecorded tapes and then tracing or pointing to the word assisted in recognition of letters, words, and phrases. Taking him through small sequential steps in reading, writing, spelling, and math, he began to succeed. Concepts already learned were included in the newly presented material. I was cautious of not using materials which Bob construed as babyish. Subjects I used to represent a concept were subjects that interested him. Upon grasping skills at the primary level, Bob was able to transfer his skills to his age and grade level. Reinforcing each step he accomplished encouraged him to keep trying. With the realization that he can succeed instead of can't, his attitude about himself and his ability to learn changed. Bob began to make an effort at all material given him.

I had Bob tell me stories about different events in his life. As he told me, I wrote them down. After he completed a paragraph, I had him read what I had printed. We then compared words from his story to the same words in other books. With spelling, we finger-spelled each word while verbalizing. After several repetitions, he then printed the word on paper once again, verbalizing the word and then each letter. He rewrote the story and was able to read it independently.

I had many meetings with his parents and his regular classroom teachers. They reinforced his learning by using the same procedures that I had used in my room. He became more confident, and therefore, more successful. This proves that consistent involvement from all people who come in contact with the student is a major factor in successful remediation of problem areas. Insistence that he was not allowed to use "I can't" instead of "I Can" changed his whole attitude toward learning and toward his perception of himself.

Reinforcement from caregivers, paraprofessionals, and professionals is extremely important to the progress of the child. I worked with a few classroom aides who refused to follow the programs I had developed for each student. Not giving the student positive feedback and encouragement, reinforced the student negatively. The student then refuse to try. Providing the person with the desire to achieve makes all the difference in whether or not they will succeed. Positive reinforcement needs to be provided from all people who come in contact with the person with learning disabilities.

People with learning disabilities very often have visual motor problems. In this case, their brain perceives the information differently and sends the wrong processed message to the muscles that require eye-hand coordination. This is the cause of children or adults not being able to copy material from the board or from other sources in a certain allotted time. This causes much frustration and embarrassment. I had my L.D. students who were having problems come to my classroom when there were no other students. They were then able to work at their own pace in a more relaxed situation.

With expressive and receptive language, many people with learning disabilities have a defeatist attitude due to the lack of ability to express themselves or understand others. By not completing their sentences for them, but by being patient and giving language cues, one can definitely help them in producing the correct word or sentence. Reinforcing their attempts to speak will change their attitude from "I can't" to "I can." This will increase their self-esteem which will enable them to better express themselves in all situations.

Families and friends of people with learning disabilities should provide much needed support and encouragement. When a person has confidence in what he does, he will succeed. When a person with learning disabilities is confronted with a question and expected to speak, they may have difficulty in organizing their words or finding the correct word. If they are given time and not pressured to answer spontaneously, they will be able to express themselves better. Feeling as if they are under pressure will usually prevent them from expressing their wants, needs, and opinions. With each case of failure in communication, their speech may become more jumbled and confusing. Since the basis of socialization is communication, this may cause a person with learning disabilities to be a social outcast or even to fail in school or at work. Speech therapy is recommended. The speech therapist follows a program that is stimulating but structured. The therapist also provides help with articulation problems.

In working with a person, my major objective is to foster success by reinforcements. When I provided either primary reinforcement (pats on backs, smiles, positive verbalization, or in some cases hugs) or secondary reinforcement (points, tokens, treats, etc.) for attempting or accomplishing a task, a person with learning disabilities seemed to respond more readily. Primary reinforcements are better to use with adults or adolescents whereas secondary reinforcements are better to use with younger people. Reinforcements aid the person to accomplish tasks that were previously thought to be impossible feats.

Besides academics, motor delays need to be addressed. Observations from all involved will best aid in determining which motor skills need to be focused upon. Occupational and physical therapists can help in developing programs. Motor skills are grouped into two types. Gross motor skills involve the large group of muscles (arms, legs, and trunk). Noted problems in gross motor skills are times that the individual appears to be clumsy, runs into things, or falls. These people have trouble in sports or activities that involve running, climbing, or jumping.

Fine motor skills include the use of small muscles (fingers, toes). Problems in this area show up in writing. Their writing is slow and sloppy. Their pencil grip is usually wrong. Teaching proper grip, not rushing to finish a writing program, and placing one's hand over the student's hand will help. Slowly phasing away from manual guidance will assist in developing independent proper writing skills.

Prior to the writing activity, I placed glue on the lines of the paper. This helped the student keep in the lines. Observing, keeping a record of the skill in question, and then testing of the problem areas will ensure proper remediation. The child can then receive special help in school and in after-school programs. If the child begins receiving remediation for his problem as soon as he enters the educational system, he will then have a greater chance of succeeding at various tasks throughout his lifetime. Caregivers should begin challenging the child with learning disabilities at an early age. By consistently succeeding, the child will gain a positive perspective toward his ability to succeed.

Adults with learning disabilities are covered under the Rehabilitation Act of 1973, and the Americans with Disabilities Act of 1990. Through this law, these people cannot be discriminated against and can receive basic opportunities and services.

Employers must make adjustments for these workers. One man, John, came to me frustrated and angry. He had difficulty in reading as he was reversing letters and words. He also had problems in expressing or receiving direction in both written and verbal forms. He had difficulty in memorizing information. Because of this, he had problems in following directions or steps in a task that he was expected to complete. These problems affected his work. He had difficulty with socialization skills in that he did not understand social cues. He often misinterpreted what people were saying.

After I showed him skills to overcome his difficulty, he began progressing. Taping, listening, and then repeating instructions assisted him in thoroughly understanding the crux of what was being said. Verbalizing out loud when he read assisted him in understanding and following directions. Writing down key words aids in retention. Repeating instructions assisted him in following verbal and written directions. John carried a notepad and wrote key words down to remember what he needed to do.

If adults need information or help concerning learning disabilities, they can search for answers to their questions through the publication National Resources for Adults with Learning Disabilities.[9] The publication advertises organizations, publications, and programs which can provide general information to meet the needs of adults.

The adult with learning disabilities usually has a great deal of stress during the process of finding a job and coping with different elements in the job. The stress mounts as the application is filled out, during the interview, and if hired, following all the required expectations of a job. An adult can develop a relationship with someone to help in times of need both at work and socially. A counselor will be advantageous for the person with learning disabilities to feel better about the task he attempts or accomplishments he achieves. There are many resources and agencies that can assist the adult with learning disabilities.

In the State Department of Vocational Rehabilitation, counselors can refer a person to free healthcare or financial support for healthcare, vocational training, counseling, housing, and programs, if needed, for the person with learning disabilities to obtain a GED or further education.

Through the Health Resource Center, sponsored by the American Council on Education, counselors will assist the person with learning disabilities to attend training schools, colleges, or universities. These organizations can help in providing recorded books and tapes.[10] Tests can be taken orally rather than in written form.

With the "I Can" attitude and having positive support, the person with learning disabilities can succeed.

---

[10] National Resources for Adults with Learning Disabilities, *What Aid Does the Government Offer?*, P. 17

ADDITIONAL REFERENCES

Organizations

Attention Deficit Information   Phone 800-366-2233
Network
10801 Rockville Pike
Needham, MA 02194

Center for Mental Health   Phone 301-443-2792
Services
Office of Consumer, Family,
and Public
Information (Helps with Cancer
victims that experience L.D.)
5600 Fishers Lane, Room 15-81
Rockville, MD 20857

Children with Attention Deficit   Phone 305-443-2792
Disorders
499 NW 70th Ave., Suite 308
Plantation, Florida 33317

Learning Disabilities Association of Phone 412-342-8077
America
4156 Library Road
Pittsburgh, Pennsylvania 15234

National Center for Learning   Phone 212-687-7211
Disabilities
381 Park Avenue South, Suite,
1420
New York, New York 10016

PERIODICALS AND PAMPHLETS

Learning Disabled Quarterly
Council of Exceptional Children
L.D. division

Learning Disabilities Research and Practice
Council of Exceptional Children
L.D. division

CAN
Council of Exceptional Children
L.D. division

Learning Disabilities: Graduate School and Careers
P. Alelman, C. Wren

Psychology Today
1-800-234-8361

BOOKS

Colleges with Programs for Students Learning Disabilities	C.Magnum & Strichard
Learning Disabilities and Your Child A Survival Handbook	L. Greene
The Survival Guide for Kids with L.D.	R. Cummings and G. Fisher
Josh: A Boy with Dyslexia	C. Janover
Different, Not Dumb	M. Marek
What Do you Mean I have Learning Disabilities	Walker and Co.
Facing Learning Disabilities in the Adult Years	Joan Shapiro and Rebecca Rich

Chapter IV

CONFUSION OF EMOTIONAL DISABILITIES

Mental confusion set in as Don tried to make sense of the different reactions from people about his lost period of time. He did not quite understand what he had just done, but he realized his actions stirred a variety of emotions among different people. Don was scared not knowing who he could trust to actually tell him of the incident that had just occurred. He had difficulty in establishing himself in an accepted social structure the majority of the time. Don was labeled emotionally disturbed.

Emotionally disturbed covers a large array of mental and emotional conditions. This disability has its basis in biological, psychological, and environmental roots. The term "psychiatric disability" is used when the emotional disturbance consistently affects basic life such as "learning, thinking, communicating, and sleeping."[11] The cure for emotional illness is comparable to a cog in a wheel. Each separate professional area of expertise works together for the betterment of the individual. My area of expertise in the mental health field was teaching.

To touch all areas of the complex life of an emotionally disturbed individual, I had conferences with the psychiatrists, counselors, parents, and other people who came in contact with that particular person. The team approach by professionals involved in the treatment of a person will have better results rather than each acting individually.

Over a period of time, the severity and duration of the conditions are dependent upon the treatment, medication, the type of therapy used, and the essential support from loved ones and friends. Changing one's attitude towards one's self, therapies, and activities is a major factor in rehabilitation.

Mental illness strikes more than twenty-two percent of our population during a period of one year.[12] Disorders can affect anyone regardless of their age or position in life. Both children and adults can be helped with the proper techniques, treatments, certain medications, support, and with the affirmation of the "I Can" attitude. Without proper treatment, a person with this disability will have a difficulties functioning in many activities. The interactions with a majority of people are often a cause of stress

---

[11] Center for Psychiatric Rehabilitation, Boston University. 1997. *What is Psychiatric Disability and Mental Illness?* p. 1 of 5.

[12] Austin Diagnostic Clinic, Psychiatry Health Library. 4/2004. *What is Mental Illness?* p. 1.

and frustration. People who have emotional disabilities may have difficulty in appropriately handling any type of change or perceived stress either in school, work, social, or home environments. Many tend to abuse alcohol or drugs. On occasion, some will talk about or have thoughts of suicide. Many will show signs of depression or have signs of indifference toward various aspects of life. During these times, contact with a professional in the mental health field is essential in addressing and remediation of the effected person.

If you or a loved one needs a therapist or a professional to talk to, there are a variety of people who could be contacted. The professionals who assist in mental health issues are psychiatrists, counselors, psychologists, and social workers. In the educational system, special education teachers certified in emotional disabilities plus the school counselor can also help in adapting to the needs of the person. There are also resources for a specific problem. The mental health division of the State Department can be of assistance. Also, primary care physicians can refer a person to a specific mental health physician.

I have worked with many parents who were not aware of different services or therapies which were available. They had no idea how to contact a professional who could assist with their particular problem. If a problem of any nature is not dealt with, especially when it first surfaces, the problem will tend to escalate. Contacts should be made to social workers, mental health specialists, or various trusted people who can guide one to the correct professional. Regardless of the type of mental illness, there are support groups in communities which can help the concerned loved ones deal with supporting, educating, and living with the emotionally disturbed.

If I observed emotional or behavioral problems as I began working with an individual, I would encourage the parents or providers to become aware that a problem existed and to follow specific suggestions in dealing with that particular problem. Dealing with all areas of the problem in the beginning is extremely important. Written records of what instigated the problems, the time of the problems, and what actually happened will aid the professional to touch the base of reality in solving the problem.

While working with babies who have disabilities, if I noted beginning emotional or behavioral problems, I encouraged the parents to accept that a problem does exist. Dependent upon the severity and type of problem, referrals were made to a professional dealing in the specific area of concern. Developing a program with all professionals who are in contact with the individual who has emotional problems is of extreme importance to ensure remediation of the problem. The title and description of professionals in the mental health fields are listed below.

The psychiatrists are doctors who diagnose and specialize in the treatment of psychiatric illnesses. They are licensed practitioners. They treat a person with proper medications and skillfully use different methods in speaking to a person about their problems. Their goal is to assist in changing a person's behavior and demeanor to one which is accepted in society. The person will then be able to function in society appropriately and to be more accepted with continuing therapy or proper medication.

The counselors, social workers, psychologists, or psychotherapists have degrees either in psychology or in related fields which provide academic, social, or psychological treatments. In a school setting, the psychologist tests prospective students for special programs. The psychologist then works with the students, teachers, and parents. Sometimes cooperation from parents may be difficult. The psychologist makes every effort to contact and work with the parents.

Sue Breen, a psychologist and a teacher for disabilities, states that if a parent or a caregiver cooperates and works with the professionals, the student will usually progress toward achieving academic, emotional, social, and behavioral goals. This concept is not only true for the educational system but also true for every facet of life involving the person with emotional disabilities.

The licensed psychotherapist or counselor has degrees with an emphasis on psychotherapy. They work with other mental health specialists. Their work consists of using a variety of methods to assist with problems. The problems consist of "depression, addiction and substance abuse, suicidal impulses, stress management, self-esteem issues, issues of aging, emotional health and family, parenting, marital or other relationship problems."[13]

The social workers supply an individual or family with solutions for their well-being. They assist in promoting and maintaining the person's or family's psychological and social well-being. Social

---

[13] WebMD with AOL Health. *How to Find a Therapist*. p. 1-2 of 3, 1996-2004.

work is not a specific therapy. The social worker may use various counseling methods to understand and assist with the problems that exist in the family. With this approach, they can provide services which aid in alleviating the problems.

My father, Bob Lorenzen, was a supervisor to a social work unit. When speaking with families, he used a rational emotive approach which helped families in dealing with the present realities of life. With this approach, he was able to help many families deal with specific problems that caused strains in everyday living. The social workers assist the families with finances, interactions, jobs, education, emotions, or behaviors.

In working with children and adults in institutions, school, and in the home areas, all the programs were coordinated between the psychologist, the nurse, the parents, the administration, the social workers, and any other agency involved with the family. Cooperation from all people involved ensured that appropriate programs were written and followed in order to address all the needs of the individual. All family members or people who have consistent interaction with a person who has emotional disabilities must be involved. Coordination of all programs from various professionals ensures a greater chance of recovery.

As an elementary special education resource teacher in a small town, I worked with a variety of ages and disabilities. Tom, an eight-year-old who had emotional disabilities, spent the majority of time in my classroom because of his inability to appropriately interact with peers and school personnel. During times when I did not have other students in the room, I gave Tom much needed individual attention. By playing with puppets, role-playing or just talking about and sharing the events in both our lives, he began conveying accounts of physical and sexual abuse from his single mother and her friends. I began logging all incidences that he had related to me. I shared these accounts with his family's social worker, school counselor, and the principal.

One day, Tom walked into my class with tears welling up in his eyes. He was reluctant to sit down. Upon questioning him, he told me that his mom whipped him with a belt. I canceled the scheduled times with my other students. Tom and I went to the principal and the school nurse. The principal, school nurse, and I discovered welts up and down Tom's back. The social worker was notified. With the logged information that I had kept along with the mental and physical condition of Tom, he was immediately taken out of the home. He was placed in a home that provided him with structure, love, and reinforcement. After a short period of time, Tom began improving in all areas. His attitude toward himself and what he could achieve had drastically changed from "I can't" to "I can."

Taking time to listen and reinforce good dialogue is the best method in encouraging feelings of competency. Being given a choice about how one behaves is a step in the right direction. In teaching, this allowed the student to be responsible for his own behavior. Being cautious of the type of response to a negative behavior has more of an influence in changing one's behavior than trying to control them. Responding to a negative behavior with anger only reinforces the negative behavior. Remaining calm and patient will contribute to defusing the unwanted behavior.

Many times, in classrooms or in home situations, I have seen different responses from teachers, staff, or caregivers concerning the student's behavior. The person who remained calm and patient had more control over the situation. On the other hand, the one who reacted angrily began losing control. Once control is lost, the process of regaining peace is time consuming and a detriment to all concerned.

There is a marked difference between having a behavior disorder and being emotionally disturbed. With a behavior disorder, the behavior is manipulative. The person makes attempts to control the situation or other people. These people are aware of what is going on and how their manipulative behavior may control what happens. They often see others as the problem, not them. They have deceptive ego strength and appear self-assured. Many times, they join subculture groups that are antisocial. Those with behavior disorders have tendencies to join gangs which display antisocial behaviors. Hostility toward authority is a predominant feeling. Many behavior disorder people find themselves in the criminal justice systems. Some adolescents I taught in a detention center lacked guilt for the crime they had committed. They had a difficult time justifying that their aversive behaviors resulted in being incarcerated. They rationalized "acceptable" reasoning for their behaviors. Many of these people joined gangs so they could feel accepted in a group regardless of the negative consequences.

In sessions with those with behavior disorders, I guided them through positive solutions to problems. When they felt they had developed their own positive solutions, they then had a tendency to follow the solution more so than if I or other people of authority told them what solution was needed. Patience is extremely important to have. Without patience, the behavior disorder person has exerted their control and is able to prevail over the situation.

On the other side, the emotionally disturbed behavior is in conjunction with a certain type of stress. Heredity and a chemical imbalance in the body also play a role in initiating emotional disturbances. Their behavior is uncontrollable and manipulative. They have a low self-image. Their moods change from depression to high movement. They have consistent conflicts or have unrealistic fears in dealing with other people. School and work achievements are inconsistent. With goals toward achievements, there may be misperceived fears, anxieties, denials, and confusion. Positive responses can be accomplished with a highly structured environment with few choices. Also, clear directions and explanations will aid in more of a positive outcome.

While teaching adolescents in a mental institution, I used a behavior modification point system. This gave them clear guidelines in what behaviors and actions were expected of them. They traded the points in for earned privileges or earned prizes. Discussions followed when either points or tokens were given or not given. Feelings were discussed about the positive or negative reinforcements.

Patience, understanding, and caring are of the utmost importance. Once again, working closely with the other professionals, and especially the caregivers, assures a positive and consistent setting. This enables the emotionally disturbed to manage stressful situations in a calm, understandable manner. When people approach the emotionally ill person with inconsistent methods of dealing with a problem, confusion sets in. When they are unsure of the guidelines or rules, they will begin reacting aversively. Confusion can, and will, stir up many other problems.

When I taught both those with a behavior disorder and the emotionally disturbed, I played either classical music or soft nature music. Playing that type of music in the background calmed the students down, enabling them to attend to tasks. In the mental institution, the soft music was turned off at the insistence of the head teacher. The students began reverting back to their aversive behaviors. When I started playing the music again, the students began attending to tasks. After listening to music during several sessions, they began picking their favorite tunes.

For a favorable learning setting, there should not be a clutter of papers hanging on the wall. The papers can divert one's attention from the actual work. Having a relaxing and calming environment promotes concentration. Burning incense promotes relaxation and also triggers the mind to relax. When speaking to caregivers of problem children, I encouraged them to create such an environment.

Families that tolerate the trials and tribulations of having an individual who has emotional disabilities living at home need to remember to have all family members involved to ensure a successful road to recovery. When the loved one begins noticing signs of improvement, it is extremely important to heed caution so that a relapse will not occur. Guidelines to help with the recovery process are outlined in the following eight steps:[14]

1. Set attainable goals to be achieved in the near future.
2. Reduce stress of everyday living.
3. Keep doors of communication open for all involved.
4. Reinforce, encourage, and support tasks which are accomplish independently.
5. Support problem-solving skills.
6. Be sensitive in not comparing the person to other people.
7. Be supportive in promoting independent use of taking prescribed medications.
8. Avoid a total relapse by being aware of and acting upon the signs that may indicate the beginning of a relapse.

Living with someone who has emotional disabilities can be financially and mentally demanding. There is financial assistance available which can aid in some of the costs of various therapies and medical programs. Government programs such as American Association for Retired Persons, Family Debt Counselor, Aid to Families with Dependent Children, and many programs in the Department of Economic Security are among the few that will

---

[14] Mental Wellness.Com. Janssen. *How You Can Help Your Loved One.* p. 1–2. 12/04/03.

provide assistance. There are support groups in many cities for a specific type of mental problem. Knowing there are other families who cope with the same problems will help.

Monitoring medication is an area which needs total attention. Caregivers should keep a notebook with names and numbers of professionals or organizations that can help if any problems arise. If all people in the living situation work together with the professionals and handle situations with a positive, consistent framework rather than a negative framework, the overall condition of the mentally disturbed individual will make marked improvements.

The family or caregivers need special allotted time for themselves. Getting away from a stressful situation helps all concerned. When needing a much deserved break, there are many different activities one can be involved in. Some type of exercise activity, like walking or jogging, aids in relaxation. Watching a funny video or movie, reading a book, sitting in a hot tub, or meditating may also help. Time for relaxation and recharging oneself is extremely important. This will relieve any pent-up anger concerning the individual care of the mentally disturbed. Getting away from a stressful situation is the best therapy for both the affected individual and the caretakers.

There are various types of labels for emotional disabilities. Three which are most common are anxiety disorders, depressive disorders, and schizophrenia. [15]

---

[15] Center for Psychiatric Rehabilitation, Boston University. *Reasonable Accommodations. What is Psychiatric Disability and Mental Illness?* 1997. p.1-5.

An anxiety disorder is the repulsive and sometimes unbearable emotion with a reaction of a perceived situation. Some of the symptoms of anxiety disorders are depression, helplessness, delusions, irrational fear, mood fluctuations, physical complaints, insomnia, perfectionism, and anger. The sub-areas are panic disorders, phobias, obsessive-compulsive disorders, and post traumatic stress.

Andree was diagnosed with a form of anxiety disorder called panic attacks. These attacks caused her to fear different events in life and perceive the outcomes pessimistically. She views many things unrealistically and with fatal outcomes. During an attack, Andree has headaches. The attacks also aggravate her essential tremors causing her hands to begin to shake uncontrollably. She predominately has an unsteady feeling. She begins sweating. Panic attacks can also cause heart palpitations, chest pains, hot and cold flashes, and faintness. Speaking in a slow, soft, steady voice helped guide her through the attacks. Having sessions with a psychiatrist assisted her in a belief that she is still an okay person. Showing support and love among the family and friends is an important factor that cannot be replaced.

Tom has an anxiety disorder called social phobia. He has a fear of interacting with people. This fear will be construed in his own mind as a cause of unreasonable persecution of himself. This causes him to avoid social situations. If Tom is placed in a social situation, he begins feeling threatened because of his misinterpretations of people's reactions toward him. Tom is gradually phasing into interactions with people. He is realizing that his opinions can be questioned but he is still an okay person. With this phobia, his loved ones need to listen to his objections, guide him through social interactions, and be very patient.

In my case, I had anxiety disorder in the form of post-traumatic stress after I was in a serious automobile accident. When I began driving after the accident, I had a difficult time fearing a vehicle approaching from a side street. This caused me to be overly cautious. I would suffer the physical symptoms of sweating and having headaches. Through the years, I convinced myself that there was no need to be frightened. Self-hypnosis and self-talking has helped remedy that problem.

Jeff has an obsessive-compulsive disorder. He painstakingly repeats a certain activity in a repetitive, identical manner. He consistently insists on perfection. He also refuses to throw away certain objects and has them neatly placed in an organized system. Throwing things away causes uncomfortable physical symptoms. He has accepted the fact of his problem and has learned to live with it. He does not let this problem affect other areas of his life.

Agoraphobia does not occur as often as the other anxiety disorders. This is a fear of being in a situation in public where escape may be difficult; for instance, being in elevators, tunnels, public bathrooms, or crowded stores. The fear could develop into a panic attack. With a trusted companion by their side talking and assuring them that all will be alright aids in helping the person feel more comfortable.

Janine suffers from agoraphobia. If her companion stays at Janine's side, talking to her and reassuring her all will be okay, she is able to handle many situations without feeling too overwhelmed. In public restrooms, her companion will stand near the door of the stall.

The cause of anxiety disorders has been recently determined to be a chemical imbalance in the brain. The emotions felt are based upon releasing or absorbing neurotransmitters in the brain. This is how the cells communicate with the body. When there are no chemicals released, or they released too slowly, depression, anxiety, or stress will occur.[16]

This chemical imbalance is caused by a deficiency in Serotonin and Norepinephrine. With the deficiency of these two chemicals, symptoms of mental illness can become a factor especially in the areas of anxiety and depression.[17]

Without Serotonin, the person can become annoyed and have experiences similar to psychotic or maniac episodes. They may have episodes of shaking or having tremors. Their blood pressure and pulse may increase. To avoid such episodes, a person needs to consume foods that have proteins. Protein-rich foods include poultry, meat, fish, soy, nuts, grains, rice, eggs, milk, or cheese. A person should not use any alcohol or caffeine several hours before bedtime.

Even though depressive disorders primarily affect the person emotionally, the person can also be affected physically. Depression

---

[16] Anxiety Disorder and Anxiety Treatment Information, *www.anxiety-and-depression-solutions.com*. 5/23/04. p. 2 of 4.

[17] Anxiety and Depression—Anxiety, Depression Treatment and Information, ibid. 6/17/04. p.2 of 5.

implicates mood changes. The person experiencing depressed states has poor self-esteem and feels they do not deserve anything. Often, they talk about or attempt suicide. People in a depressive state tend to lose interest or enjoyment. Their attitudes toward objects, people, and events are negative. Their appetites will vary by either over-eating or under-eating. There will be significant weight gain or loss. Depression affects sleep patterns and usually causes insomnia. They also can wake up during the night and have problems returning back to sleep.

With proper medication and treatment, there can be a marked improvement in the majority of people with depression. There are many prescription drugs to help defeat the effects of depression. Some of the prescribed drugs are Valium, Prozac, Paxil, Xanax, Nardil, and Zoloft. Often, with these drugs, people experience blurred vision and have a temporary solution to the problem. If the medication is not taken, they can revert back to their depressed state. Clarocet NRI, which has relieved people of the effects of depression, is a natural medicine.[18] It balances the neurotransmitters in the brain.

There are natural therapies that have been reported to help people with their problem of depression. There are subliminal audio tapes to reprogram the sub and super-conscious to react to various stimuli in a more appropriate manner or be able to eradicate an unwanted behavior or habit. These tapes have soft music along with hidden meanings which one cannot hear

---

[18] *Anxiety and Depression Information Page.*, http://anxiety-and-depression-solutions.com, 7/1/04, p, 3

consciously. Subliminal tapes are based upon the fact that the sub and super-conscious controls you mentally and physically. Hypnosis is another natural remedy which aids in controlling the sub and super-conscious. Counseling or psychotherapy, along with these methods, can aid in a person feeling better and becoming more relaxed about himself and his therapies.

Schizophrenia is an extremely complex mental illness. This illness is usually developed as a teenager up to the middle twenties. With this illness, thoughts are fragmented and reactions to people and events are misconstrued.

Questions have been raised about the actual cause of schizophrenia. The cause seems to be attributed to either genetic factors or to a chemical or structural imbalance in the brain. There are several characteristics that indicate schizophrenia. These symptoms are grouped into positive or negative signs.

Positive signs include delusions, seeing and hearing things, speech which is unrelated to the topic of conversation, exaggerated and inappropriate emotions, erratic facial and body movements, and not attending to self-hygiene.

Negative signs include withdrawal from society, varied and different emotions that are usually displayed during certain situations, no desire to accomplish tasks, and showing no emotions in speech patterns.

Without professional help, withdrawal from society can be the only comforting resource for a person, especially when they have difficulty in relating to and understanding the "whys" of both the common laws and formal laws of society.

Some people who have an emotional disorder may inappropriately blurt out words or passages. Emotions which do not fit the scenario may be present. Outbursts of anger for no apparent reason may occur. Sometimes, the person may not show any emotion regardless of what is occurring around them.

There are a group of people who have delusions, hallucinations, and thought disorders. Delusions are beliefs that are illogical but seem logical in the affected person's mind. When working in a library at a mental institution, Don and I had discussions of travel, culture, and languages around the world. We would be in the middle of a stimulating conversation when he would hesitate. With a fearful look in his eyes, he would try to convince me that a certain group is hiding in the library, taking notes of his conversation, and getting ready to use aversive means to harm him. He then would continue where he left off in our conversation as if he had no fears. I would continue the conversation with him and make a mental note of our interruption which I would relate to the professionals who worked with him.

With hallucinations, the person insists on perceiving things that are not real; for example, listening to voices of imaginary people. I have noted a few people on the street having conversations with imaginary people. I also notice "normal" people pointing at them and laughing. These people should not be made fun of. They truly believe in the nonexistent person. Laughing or making an issue of their confused state only aggravates the situation.

Thought disorder comes about when a person does not follow the subject of conversation and begins blurting out completely different topics or words. Following discussions thoroughly can be a difficult feat for them. I have been in social situations where I had to remind the person of the topic of conversation. These people need to be the center of attention or think that their ideas are appropriate at the time.

Keeping situations from becoming stressful is one of the major factors in helping the person with emotional disabilities. Even though a person may be aware of the cause of the problem, they have difficulty in controlling the symptoms. Patience and a quiet supportive voice will help guide the person through the problem.

Regardless of the type of therapy and medication administered to a person with an emotional disability, having a positive and calm attitude will promote a quicker road to recovery.

ADDITIONAL REFERENCES

Organizations

American Psychological Association   Phone: 800-374-2721
750 1st St. NE
Washington D.C. 20002-4242

National Mental Health Association   Phone: 800-950-6264
Colonial Place Three   703-524-9094
2107 Wilson Blvd, Suite 300   Fax: 703-524-9094
Arlington, VA 22201-3042

National Federation of Families for
Children's Mental Health   Phone: 703-684-7710
1101 King St., Ste. 420   Fax: 703-836-1040
Alexandria, VA 22314

U.S. Dept. of Health and Human Services   Phone: 301-458-4000
For Disease Control and Prevention   Fax: 703-524-9094
Hyattsville, MD 20782

National Mental Health Information Center   Phone: 800-789-2647
U.S. Department Of Health and Human   TDD: 866-889-2647
Services
Substance Abuse and Mental Health   Fax: 240-747-5475
Service
P.O. Box 42557
Washington D.C. 20015

The American Academy of Child &   Phone: 202-966-7300
Adolescent Psychiatry   3615
Wisconsin Ave, N.W.   Fax: 240-747-5470
Washington D.C. 20015

Periodicals and Newsletters

Psychology Today	800-234-8361
Journal of Family Psychology	202-336-5600
Self-Help Magazine	www.selfhelpmagazine.com
Humanist	202-238-9088

BOOKS

Understanding and Teaching   Phyllis L. Newcomer
Emotionally Disturbed Children
and Adolescents

Responding to an Emotionally   Laurie Cyr-Mariel
Disturbed Person
A Manual for Law Enforcement
Personnel

Characteristics of Emotional and   James Kauffman
Behavioral
Disorders of Children and Youth

Defiant Child: A Parent's Guide to   Douglas Riley
Oppositional Defiant Disorder

Chapter V

SILENT WORLD OF THE HEARING IMPAIRED

A hard-of-hearing or deaf person may have many problems deriving from their inability to hear some or all of the sounds. This could lead to difficulty in normal daily activities and can have debilitating effects upon any individual regardless of their mental capacity. Throughout the remainder of this chapter, the term "hearing-impaired" refers to both hard-of-hearing and total deafness unless otherwise indicated.

Without having a thorough basis in language and communication skills, the hearing impaired person may be perceived as functioning at a lower intellectual level. For example, when taking a group of hearing impaired children out to a public event, people would become very impatient with them. The hearing impaired children were attempting to communicate either verbally or in written form. People would over-articulate their speech. Raised eyebrows and strange looks would be a common occurrence. Some people mimicked the hearing impaired persons use of sign language. Snide remarks and would be heard and sometimes seen. To demean the hearing impaired, physical and verbal connotations were used the majority of the time.

Life-training skills, the proper hearing aid amplification, training in speech reading, awareness of body language and communication either in speech, sign language or both are required to offset the effects of the hearing loss. Lacking these skills, the consequences are low self-esteem, isolation, social immaturity, a sense of rejection, and hesitancy to socialize with both hearing and non-hearing people.

A major factor in the psychosocial realm is the amount of positive interaction from the intermediate family or caregiver and also from the general public. The type and degree of hearing loss may affect the hearing impaired negatively if they do not have a good positive support system and professional training.

One young boy, Mike, whom I taught in a public school, had severe hearing loss. Even though he had no professional training in communication skills, his father and mother consistently involved him positively in all aspects of their lives. These special parents took time to include their son in many different types of activities. They always explained the events to Mike by using speech, a few signs in American Sign Language and Signed English, and body language, especially facial expressions. During any type of interaction with Mike, these parents provided him with love and special guidance. Through consistent observation, the parents were very aware of whether or not Mike understood the situations. He was made to feel very important to his family and worthy of people that he came in contact with. He had a good self-esteem. At times, when peers or adults made crude gestures or comments, Mike was able to deal with these episodes. He had learned that when people had difficulty with his deafness that it was their problem, not his. He learned to either ignore people on occasion or to explain to them while teaching them that despite his deafness, he was no different than hearing children. When Mike did have problems, he confided in his parents and they lovingly guided him through any situation.

By the time Mike was in second grade, he had good self-esteem. He had an excellent foundation in understanding receptive language. His expressive language was composed of mouthing an approximation of words or pointing. Once he learned expressive and receptive sign language and some speech, he progressed remarkably in all areas of life. His parents worked closely with the teachers and therapist. They coordinated the lessons from school and therapy with happenings in the home. Mike easily blended into all activities at home, school, and in society.

On the other hand, I worked with a moderately hearing impaired two-year-old, Carol, who had no stimulation from people in her home environment. Even though this child seemed to be observing what was happening in daily activities, Carol remained in an infant-like state. As a parent advisor, I demonstrated to the family the importance of positive interaction with Carol, regardless of the activity or lesson being implemented. The family did not smile, hug, or show any signs of love. The family attempted to use some sign language, but unfortunately, their attempts were infrequent. There was no consistency in the use of her hearing aid. Carol would either throw her aid in the toilet or hide it. The family did not reprimand her. Because of this failure, Carol had very few communication skills. Self-help skills that were demonstrated were very seldom implemented.

When the negative interactions superseded the positive ones, Carol was removed from her negative home environment and placed in a stimulating foster home. The new people in Carol's life responded to her presymbolic communication which was her way of communicating through tears, body movements, and eye contact. Logical and realistic expectations, sensory skills, auditory development including the consistent use of a hearing aid, self-help skills, and receptive and expressive language were presented consistently in a positive manner. She began progressing in all areas. Her new family provided her with love, attention, and positive reinforcements with each small step toward attaining her goals. The positive interactions toward Carol's responses to academic and nonacademic issues increased her awareness and excitement of life. This young child changed from a totally inactive person to an active happy person.

Adults and older children who have become hearing impaired after they have led a life of being able to hear sounds need just as much support and love from the significant people in their lives. Their acceptance of their disability can largely be shaped by the reaction of friends, loved ones, and people in their surroundings. These people need to feel that despite their hearing problem, they are basically an okay person. While following the training of a therapist, a hearing specialist, an audiologist, doctors, and counselors, they can succeed and continue living their lives as normally as possible.

Coco has recently had a hearing loss in one ear. She is a very active person. She enjoys having conversations with many different types of people. She now has difficulty in following all conversations because of the lack of hearing. This causes much frustration and embarrassment at times. Coco has a difficult time admitting to herself and others that she has a hearing problem. Love and family support has assisted her to some degree in accepting her deafness. At times such as this, meeting reality head-on will help in developing an acceptance to the problem. Counseling may be justified in situations similar to this.

When interacting with the hearing impaired, regardless of the situation or age, a conscientious effort to abide by the following guidelines will aid in more of a relaxed and optimistic interaction.

1. The hearing impaired person must see your lips.
2. Do not stand in front of windows while talking. The light should shine on your face, and not the hearing impaired persons' eyes.
3. Do not cover your face, especially your mouth, when speaking.
4. Do not over-exaggerate words or speak in a slower mannerism. Speak naturally.
5. Do not move around when speaking.

6. Throughout the conversation, ask the hearing impaired if he understands or has questions on what is being said.

7. Attempt to ask the sign for specific words and use these signs when appropriate.

8. Ask the hearing impaired his opinions of the topic being discussed.

9. Use facial expressions and body movements to describe feelings.

10. If you do not understand what the hearing impaired is signing, ask questions about the subject. Do not pretend to understand what the hearing impaired is conveying.

There are various types of hearing loss.[19] The type of hearing loss will determine the type of treatment and will be a significant factor upon determining communication problems.

Difficulty in the outer part of the ear is called conductive hearing loss. The problem can be generated by the following middle ear problems: excessive wax in the ear canal, fluid in the middle ear, or a broken ossicle bones which make a connection between the eardrum and inner ear. This hearing loss possibly could be corrected by a physician.[20]

Sensorineural hearing loss is permanent and a hearing aid is essential. Sensorineural loss is caused by problems in the inner

---

[19] Ski Hi Curriculum. Property of the Parent Outreach Program for the Hearing-Impaired. "Anatomy of The Ear," p. 166-167.

[20] All information included on pages 95-103 is derived from papers and lectures for Parent Advisors in Arizona, 1983-2003,

ear or with the auditory nerve. Some problems of this type are generated by the absence of a cochlea, imperfections in the ear during prenatal developments, drugs, loud sounds, or heredity. Despite these known causes, there are still unknown causes for this loss.

Mixed hearing loss is partially sensorineural and partially conductive. The primary cause of this loss is due to fluid in the middle ear.

Central auditory deficits are problems in the brainstem or the auditory nerve. These problems can be caused by bleeding or a blood clot in the brain, a tumor, or diseases such as meningitis. Although this problem is not as obvious as the other hearing impaired problems, it still can affect the person's ability to process language.

When a person is suspected of having hearing loss, he may be sent to an otolaryngologist or an otologist who are physicians that have an understanding of diseases of the ear, nose, and throat. Otolaryngologist responsibilities are to evaluate a person's hearing loss and suggest appropriate medical consideration. The otologist is a physician who specializes in problems of the ear. The Federal Trade Commission mandated that approval from these physicians is necessary before purchasing a hearing aid.

If hearing loss is suspected, the patient is referred to an audiologist. He has the responsibility for testing the hearing and determining the person's actual degree of hearing.

There are several types in hearing tests for both children and adults. The type of test is determined usually by the age and the type of hearing problem the person complains of having. After the tests, the audiologist will record the results of the test on an audiogram. After collecting the results, the audiologist will determine if a person will benefit from having a hearing aid.

The audiologist records the loudness or intensity (decibels) and pitch (frequencies) of hearing on an audiogram. The intensity or loudness is indicated by the numbers going down the audiogram. The word for these numbers is decibel (dB). As the number increases, the loudness increases. The pitch or frequencies are written across the audiogram. This represents the number of cycles of sound waves in one second. This is named hertz (Hz). The 0 and X show what was heard through the earphones. This is called "air conduction." Speech sounds can vary in dB and Hz. The classification of loss is indicated by the following in decibels: 0-10 normal, 11-25 borderline or minimal, 26-45 mild, 46-65 moderate, 66-85 severe, and 85+ profound. The amount of decibels could vary a bit according to different charts.

Regardless of whether a child or an adult has minimal, mild, moderate, severe, profound, or unilateral hearing loss, their dealings and interactions with the primary people in their lives will have a profound effect upon their interactions with other people in all situations.

People with a borderline or minimal hearing loss may have difficulty hearing soft or distant speech. They could miss parts of a fast-paced conversation. Because of having to intensively listen to conversations, they tire more easily. Assist them if they become confused. Speak at a normal rate. Include them in the conversation. Look at them while speaking.

With a mild hearing loss, a person can miss twenty-five to forty percent of speech sounds. The amount of speech actually missed can be dependent upon the noise level in the immediate environment. The speaker must be conscious of being in direct view of the hearing impaired person. Be patient and ensure that the hearing impaired person is not left out of the conversation by not being able to comprehend certain words. Speak in the ear that has less loss.

When a person has moderate hearing loss, a FM system can be used. FM systems will pick up the voice signals of the person who is speaking in the microphone, intensify the voice, and transmit it to the listener. Unwanted sounds are overcome by supplying a direct line of communication by the two people involved. Hearing aids in all situations are essential. The hearing impaired person may be thought of as not paying attention to conversations. The person may have limited vocabulary or a deficit in speech formation involving both the syntax of language and the various productions of sounds. Self-esteem can be affected. Hesitancy to interact with others is a common occurrence. Including and supporting them are the best ways to effectively help the moderately hearing impaired person.

A necessity for a person with severe hearing loss is the use of an amplification system usually in the form of a hearing aid. Without the aid, they can hear voices only a few feet away. If the deafness occurs prior to learning speech and language, there will be a delay in the formation of sounds and in the production of a sentence. This group feels more comfortable interacting with other hearing impaired people.

When meeting a person with a severe hearing loss, allow time for them to communicate through writing. If understanding their speech is difficult, do not pretend to understand. Ask questions or ask them to write down what they want to express. Do not make comments indicating that they are dumb. Most can read lips. Respect them.

Respect their abilities and opinions. The attitude of the caregiver and people who interact with the child or adult with severe hearing loss must be supportive, loving, and positive.

With profound hearing loss, a person has gained more awareness in the use of their other senses. They can pick up on visual or touch cues more often than their hearing peers. They become more conscious of vibrations that are created from sounds. Because of the lack of hearing, the person with profound hearing loss may have trouble communicating, interacting, and adjusting to a hearing world. Training for adjustment to the hearing world must begin at the onset of the hearing problem. When the children I worked with began their training soon after the discovery of their hearing loss, they had fewer problems in adjusting to their lack of sound. They usually made great strides toward their independence.

Unilateral hearing loss involves normal hearing in one ear and a permanent mild hearing loss in the other. The speaker needs to be conscious of being near the good ear when speaking. Listening is difficult when the surrounding area is noisy. Noise level should be kept at a minimum.[21]

There are different kinds of hearing aids. In-the-canal aids fit either partially or completely in the ear canal. This aid is usually used for people who have good manual dexterity or have assistance with the daily placement of the aid. These aids cannot be seen. In-the-ear aids fit completely in the outer part of the ear. These are bigger than the in-the-canal aid.

Behind-the-ear aids are enclosed in a small case. A piece of tubing with an ear mold at the end is attached to the hearing aid. Younger children are fitted with these types of aids more frequently. With the advancement in technology, there are now aids which have microchips. These aids are programmed by an audiologist to be set for various listening environments such as the quietness of home, hustle of a restaurant, or the loudness of a shopping area. In some aids, the hearing setting can be programmed by pushing a button on the hearing aid.

Regardless of the classification of hearing loss, positive parent or guardian or family support is of the utmost importance for the welfare of the hearing impaired child or even the hearing impaired adult. Also, knowledge and understanding of all areas of hearing loss is important for the hearing impaired and their loved one. The child who feels comfortable and safe in his immediate environment will progress.

---

[21] Karen L. Anderson, Ed. S and Noel D. Matkin, PhD. *Relationship of Degree of Long-term Hearing Loss to Psychosocial Impact and Educational Needs.* Presented at Parent Outreach Program Seminar in 1991.

In the beginning, the wearing of a hearing aid should only be used in short time increments. Objects or people that produce loud sounds should be avoided if possible. A first-time user of aids should gradually be introduced to a number and variety of sounds. This method will enable a person to focus or localize more easily upon essential sounds.

When I first began working with an infant or young child, I encouraged the parents to keep the noise level at a minimum. Using this method enticed the child to accept the hearing aid. Without slowly phasing into wearing an aid, the child will become very resistant to using an aid. With an older person, listening, being patient, and being respectful will aid the recently effected hearing impaired person to adapt more readily to their new circumstances.

When a person begins to wear an aid, especially young children, teach them to localize or discover what is making the sound. By showing the object producing a specific sound, the person will then be able to familiarize them with that sound and will be able to focus just on that particular object. Choices of activities familiarizing a person with a sound are dependent upon when the deafness first occurred and upon the mental capabilities of the person. With hearing aids, a person may hear sounds that they have not heard in a long time or sounds they have never heard. Your voice and voices of others will seem louder. The audiologist can provide orientation into the use of the hearing aid.

With a young child, play games in which listening experiences can be achieved. For example, have two or three sound-making toys placed next to each other. While the child is watching, produce the sound of the toy by squeezing, pulling a string, or turning a key, etc. Have the child then create the sound by the same method. Turn the child around, with his or her back facing the toy. Create the noise of one toy, then point to your ear and with a quizzical look on your face ask the child which toy made the noise. As with any learning experience, reinforce the child as the correct answer is given. If the child does not respond or gives the wrong answer, gently guide him through producing the sounds again. This may need to be repeated several times. Remind him to listen. Take walks with the child and point out various items that produce sounds. Demonstrate the sign and verbalize the name of the item. Also discuss if the sound is loud or faint. Hearing activities should be encompassed in all areas of daily living.

The care and maintenance of the hearing aid is extremely important. When the hearing aid is not in use, remove the batteries. When batteries are not producing the desired sound, change them. Removing the batteries at night is useful. Boxes of batteries should be kept in the refrigerator. Keep on hand a battery tester. A person should not sleep, bathe, or swim while wearing their hearing aid. Hearing aids should be protected from sand, heat, moisture, or any physical abuse. When children begin wearing an aid, teach them at an early age the responsibilities of caring for their aids. Clean the case, receiver, and cords with a damp cloth only. Ear molds can be washed with warm water and soap. Heed special caution to dry the ear mold. Replacing the tubing and cords at specific intervals will help maintain the hearing aid. Keep the prongs on the cord clean. If corroded, a damp cloth dipped in baking soda will remove the deposit. When the hearing aid is not in use, put it in a safe, dry place. Be very careful not to drop the transmitter. Do not let the transmitter be exposed to heat. Taking care of a hearing aid is essential for the optimal condition of the aid and for ideal assistance with communication.

A cochlear implant is a small apparatus which is surgically implanted in the cochlea of the inner ear. Through this mechanism, the auditory nerves are stimulated to send "messages" to the brain which enables the deaf person to hear. Once the cochlear implant is placed in the ear, the hearing impaired person will go through rehabilitation to adjust to a hearing world. This technique is consistently being improved.[22]

Productive interaction with a deaf person can usually be established by learning to communicate in deaf sign language. It is of the utmost importance to respect and communicate in the type of sign a specific deaf person uses.

Even though there are different kinds of sign language, the deaf mainly communicate in an American Sign Language (ASL) format. This format has its own grammar, syntax, and rules. It is a visual-gestural-spatial language. Body movement, facial expressions, and placement of the hands are intricate parts of this language. ASL is considered by the deaf as their native language. This language has all the fundamental elements of a true language. It does contain both general and abstract concepts and thoughts. Even though

---

[22] The Canadian Hearing Society. *Deaf Employee.* p. 3.

many hearing people have opinions of this language as being a crude system of broken English, this fact was proven wrong. This is widely used among the deaf and the deaf advocates throughout Canada and the United States. Just as in spoken English, there are different signs or gestures for certain idioms in various parts of the region. Deaf people in other countries have established their own specific signs, but basically follow the signs of American Sign Language. The basic ASL principles are listed below.

1) Time indicators come first because verbs remain in present tense.
2) The topic discussed is presented first followed by a comment which describes or tells about the topic.
3) Nouns are usually presented before adjectives.
4) There are directional verbs which use one sign indicating the action of the nouns without using the noun names of whom or what were involved.
5) The "wh" question words are at the end of the sentence.
6) Voice tones are symbolized by body movements or facial expressions.
7) The use of the sight line is an imaginary line running from the signer to the observer. Pointing within the sight line can be used to refer to people, things, places, and events.

Total communication includes many forms of communication. The forms are speech, lip-reading, formal signs, gestures, finger-spelling, writing, and reading. Other types of sign language which are related to this form are as follows: Manual Coded English is a term to include Signed English (Siglish), Seeing Essential English (SEE I), Signing Exact English (SEE II), Linguistics of Visual English (Love). Because of the correct English syntax, conjugation of verbs, the use of articles, the hearing impaired feel that these are the hearing people's signs. These signs take a longer time to communicate a concept.

Pidgin sign language is the use of lip-reading, finger-spelling, and ASL signs. Finger-spelling represents single hand positions for the twenty-six letters in the alphabet. Users of the Pidgin language have developed speed while communicating. Shortcuts have been developed to decrease the time of communicating. For example, when spelling a word which has a double letter, either move that letter in an up-down movement or just eliminate one of the letters. Words consisting of few letters are finger-spelled.

The Rochester Method is an oral multisensory method. This form uses the receptive skill of speech reading and is supplemented by finger-spelling and auditory amplification. Signs are not used in this method. Auditory amplification is the use of a product that amplifies sounds like the Phonic Ear or hearing aids.

Whichever type of communication a hearing impaired person uses, the receiver should respect and attempt to communicate in the format that was first presented. When I taught sign language at a junior college level, I taught Signing Exact English for my beginning class. Teaching SEE sign first assisted my students in having a good basis in vocabulary without worrying about learning a new syntax. However, throughout the class sessions, I taught the difference in the signs and structure between American Sign Language and Signing Exact English. In the intermediate class, I taught just ASL. My college students comfortably communicated with the hearing impaired. Practice is essential to have fluency in sign.

There are two options in the use of a phone for the hearing impaired. The ones who have enough hearing can use the phone, especially if they are familiar with the person they are communicating with. They need to be cautious of not putting the pressure of the phone on their hearing aid. Using a "T" switch on some hearing aids will make understanding of phone conversations easier. Digital hearing aids can be programmed for the phone.

The hearing impaired also can use a telecommunication device (TTY). This device has a keyboard and small screen in which messages can be typed.

Both the sender and receiver needs to have a TTY. Computers are widely used.

There are many devices to make the hearing impaired person's life at home easier. There are systems to indicate if there is a phone call or the doorbell rings. The hearing impaired is alerted by flashing lights or loud sounds that can be heard. By setting specific times on alarm clocks, the hearing impaired can be signaled either by a bright flashing light or the pillow or bed will be engineered to vibrate. Many television sets now have a caption decoder, which displays the text of what is being said. Through this, the hearing impaired is able to enjoy many programs. There are also devices which visually alert parents if their child is crying or there is smoke in the house.[23]

Many public schools have hearing impaired children included in regular classrooms with the assistance of a special education teacher or teacher of the deaf checking on the progress of the child. Sign language interpreters are available. The interpreter must be certified and able to communicate in sign language at the level in which the student can understand. The FM system is a system which helps the hearing impaired distinguishes the teacher's voice from other sounds in the classroom. The other students will feel more comfortable if they have some knowledge of deafness. Having a specialist on hearing impairment speak and answer questions before the hearing impaired student enters the classroom will ease any tension or curiosity other students may have. Having the students learn some sign language will aid in breaking the barrier of communication. Caution the other students not to use the word "dumb" when speaking of deafness. The hearing impaired student should sit in front of the classroom where they can see the lip movement of the teacher. When speaking to the hearing impaired, look directly at them.

Colten was one of the deaf children I worked with as a parent advisor. His parents exceeded the parental guidelines for the psychological, emotional, educational, and communication needs of their deaf child. This family moved to Tucson, Arizona from a small town which did not provide Colten with stimulating educational

---

[23] David Deyo. *Growing Together.* Galludet University, 1987

and social experiences. In Tucson, Colten was eventually placed into a class of hearing and non hearing children. In this class, all students were taught and encouraged to communicate in sign language and speech. Colten is now able to comfortably interact with both hearing impaired and hearing people. This is an ideal setting for both hearing and hearing impaired children.

Since there are many hearing impaired people in society, having the hearing impaired in class is the beginning of teaching students how to interact and relax with a variety of people. Having a responsible student assisting the hearing impaired with any questions that may arise with oral class work or in interacting with others will benefit the hearing impaired student and will ensure the smoothness of class activities.

Sounds vibrate off of surfaces creating an echo effect. This is called reverberation. To secure a good learning setting for the hearing-impaired, the classroom or even rooms in a house or on a job need to be designed to where the vibration of sound is minimal. Carpeting floors or covering walls with paper or material will help. Maintaining electrical equipment will help in not producing unwanted noise. With a few considerations toward the hearing impaired, the various environments can be an advantage, not a disadvantage, to the hearing impaired.

The hearing impaired person can find employment in many settings with the aid of interpreters, hearing aids, or even the FM system. Hiring the hearing impaired is covered under the Americans with Disabilities Act in the Rehabilitation Act Section 504. There are many ideal jobs such as teachers for the hearing impaired, teaching sign language, communicating in sign language in hospital settings or public settings, and various work situations which do not involve using the telephone and are not based upon communication skills. A hearing impaired employee is eligible for an interpreter. The interpreter must be certified. Their job is to translate the communication needs of both the hearing impaired and the hearing person in a clear, concise manner. In the United States, the interpreter must be fluent in American Sign Language. Interpreters are also used at schools, including programs of higher learning, meetings, job interviews, appointments, churches, social functions, plays, and movies.

The hearing impaired person can function equally with their hearing counterparts in all areas of life, including social, learning and work situations. They require support from concerned ones. They need proper training to deal with an environment that caters to the hearing. This includes training with various amplification methods and communication skills.

Not unlike any hearing person, the hearing impaired can accomplish and meet the expectations of many jobs. The physical ability to use specialized equipment, the intelligence required for a specific job and the "I Can" positive attitude applies to all. All workers require training. In the case of some of the hearing impaired, a qualified interpreter is required, not unlike non-English speaking people.

ADDITIONAL REFERENCES

Organizations

National Association of the Deaf

814 Thayer Ave
Silverspring, MD 20910-4500
Email NADinfo@nad.org

Phone (Voice)301-587-1788
(TTY) 301-587-1789
Fax 301-587-1791

Alexander Graham Bell Association
for the Deaf and Hard-of-Hearing
3417 Volta Place, NW
Washington D.C. 20007-2778

Phone (Voice and TTY)
202-337-5220
Email: agbell.org

American Society for Deaf Children
PO Box 3355
Gettysburg, PA 17325

Phone (Voice and TTY)
717-334-7922
Email
asdc@deafchildren.org

Self-Help for Hard of Hearing

7910 Woodmont Ave.

Phone (Voice) 301-607-2248 People
(TTY) 301 6537-2249
Fax 301-913-941

Bethesda, MD 20814
National Institute on Deafness and
Other Communication Disorders
 55 North 30th St

Omaha, NE 68131-9909

Phone 800-320-1171

E-mail
NIDCD@boystown.org

PERIODICALS AND WEBSITES

NAD News and Advocacy	Published by National Association for the Deaf
Deaf Community News	http:/www.disoez.com/ deafness.htm
Deaf News Update	http://www/ deafworldministries.com/news. htm
Employment for Deaf/H.H	www.hiredeaf.com
Silent Word Update	Phone: 800-651-8292 (V/TTY)
Silent Word Media Resources, Inc. *7400 W. Augusta Blvd. #24-s* *River Forest, Illinois 60305-1499*	http://www.silentword.com/ update

BOOKS

Deaf Plus: A Multicultural Perspective	Editor: Kathee Christensen
Raising and Educating a Deaf Child	Mark Markschank
The Signing Family: What Every Parent Should Know About Sign Communication	David Stewart and Barbara Luetke-Stahlman
Deaf Like Me	James Spradley
A Quiet World	David Myers
Living With Deafness	Emma Haughton
Legal Rights: The Guide for Deaf And Hard-of-Hearing People	The National Association of the Deaf Law Center National Association of Deaf Department of Government Affairs

Chapter VI

TRYING TIMES OF MULTIPLE DISABILITIES

Multiple disabilities can be comprised of a combination of two or more of the following areas: mental, emotional, neurological, muscular, physical, behavioral, and sensory impairment. These people are usually affected to such a degree that there are consequences from the multiple symptoms that affect the person in academic, work, social, and everyday life.

Multiple disabilities must be regarded as two different entities for programming, services, and therapy. The multiple symptoms can be generated by one main disease or disability. For example, during an attack of multiple sclerosis, a person may have trouble with memory loss, attention span, and blurry, foggy, or hazy vision. These symptoms do not indicate mental disabilities or visual impairment, but observers often mistakenly label the person as such. On the other side, a person can actually be afflicted with two or more completely separate disabilities which coincide. For example, a person can have both hearing disabilities and visual impairment. These disabilities are not related to a primary disease like multiple sclerosis.

When a person's disabilities are generated by one major affliction, then the symptoms of the primary affliction should be attended to first. If a person has two separate disabilities, then each disability must be addressed. The disability which creates the biggest challenge should be the primary focus.

Physical impairments usually appear with people who have multiple disabilities. Physical impairments involve the loss of functions with independent movement. There are a variety of physical impairments that vary in type and intensity. The physical impairments are neurological impairments, cerebral palsy, multiple sclerosis, muscular dystrophy, neurological impairments, monoplegia (involves one limb), hemiplegia (involves one side), quadriplegia (involves all four limbs), and arthritis.

People with multiple disabilities require extensive therapy from a variety of specialists. Coordinating the different programs will enable the person with multiple disabilities to be integrated into society with fewer problems than anticipated. As soon as a person is diagnosed with multiple disabilities, programs must begin. There are early childhood programs which will enable the parents to adapt to their child's disabilities and assist their child to succeed in primary goals affecting different areas of life. When an adult is diagnosed with multiple disabilities, there are counseling and support groups which can help psychologically and physically in adapting to the disease.

As a parent advisor for the Outreach Program for the deaf, blind, and multiple disabilities, I began working with infants. This program allowed me to assist the parents in all areas of development of their child.

One small child, Niki, had mental and physical disabilities, and was hearing impaired . Niki progressed rapidly because of the follow through of all programs by the parents. She now is achieving and improving continually in a regular classroom. Early intervention programs had supported the parents and Niki. This provided Niki with the means to developmentally grow.

Regardless of the amount or kind of disabilities that a person has, the primary concern is to gain that person's trust prior to any type of therapy, teaching, or interaction. Establishing a rapport creates a good therapeutic relationship. Any person, regardless of the disabilities, age, or mental capacity will attempt many undertakings if they have a positive rapport and respect for the person who is guiding or assisting them. This has been quite evident in the various places I have worked. When a person is talked down to, treated younger than their age, or has been treated rudely or roughly, then they will not respond to the tasks at hand.

Sherri, the adolescent I mentioned in other chapters, with whom I had the fortunate experience of working, had multiple disabilities. She had hearing disabilities, mental retardation, cerebral palsy and had seizures.

Cerebral palsy is a disability caused by an injury to the brain either just before birth or soon after. This disease is caused by lack of oxygen to the fetus, or baby, an accident in the early years of life, lead poisoning, or child abuse.[24] Cerebral palsy can be the cause of mental disability, hearing or visual impairment, difficulty in gross motor skills, or seizures.

When Sherri had seizures, I encouraged all people around her to remain calm. People needed to keep their distance from Sherri. Furniture or objects near her were taken away. No instrument was placed in her mouth nor did anybody restrain her. If available, medical personnel were notified. Once Sherri became aware of her surroundings, I would speak to her and rub the back of her neck. After a seizure, Sherri was physically and mentally tired. I would find a place where there was no or very little visual stimulation. I then would have her rest.

Sherri was labeled with severe mental retardation. Her parents were loving, caring, and wanted the best for her. Her parents and I contacted each other continually about Sherri's programs. When Sherri was at home, they followed all school and therapy programs.

When I began working with Sherri, nobody had taught her communication. Since communication is the basis for life's activities, Sherri was left out of many activities at the institution. Because of not understanding what was going on and being left out, she aggressed. This was her only way of communicating to staff that she wanted to be recognized. Since she was violent toward herself and others, the staff's only alternative was to use a passive restraint

---

[24] Disability Resource Centre of BC. *Neurological Disabilities.* June 1, 2005 from www.drnbc.org/neurological.efm, p. 1.

approach to calm her down. This solved the short-term problems, but it did not get to the true nature of what was troubling her.

I began working with Sherri on a one-to-one basis. When she realized that her aggressive behavior would not turn me away, we began developing a rapport. We began working on communication skills, using speech and sign language. We began with single words for items she needed or had in her immediate environment. I began with the word "drink." I first showed her a glass of juice. I signed "drink" and then I had a sip. I asked her if she wanted a drink. In order for Sherri to understand what I was saying, I showed her the glass, and pointed to her with a questioning look, then again, I pointed to the glass. When she reached out for the glass, I manually guided her hand to sign "drink." After just a few times, she caught on to the idea. When she first signed drink, I gave her a drink immediately. Sherri was laughing and smiling so much that she was unable to drink. Sherri began progressing in all areas. Because of initiating the beginning of communication skills and trust, we were able to work on areas that were thought to be impossible for Sherri. We worked on her fine and gross motor skills, self-help skills, basic housekeeping, and even a few academic skills.

For fine motor skills, I had her squeeze different-sized Nerf balls. This was fun, plus instrumental in increasing fine motor skills. This exercise also provided a basic lesson in counting. As she squeezed the Nerf ball, I counted in speech and sign. I then showed her four fingers and counted. I squeezed the Nerf ball four times simultaneously with counting out loud. I gave the ball to

Sherri and encouraged her to mouth the word for the numbers. We eventually progressed to counting up to twenty.

We went on many walks. Lessons incorporated into walking included receptive and expressive language, some academics, fine and gross motor skills, and most importantly, a chance to be by ourselves and develop a very important student teacher relationship. Prior to our walks, we looked at a picture of simple houses and pictures of people and animals. On some of the walks, we picked up different-sized sticks. With pictures I carried, I pointed to a simple picture of a house or people. I pointed to Sherri and then at me. I then pointed to the sticks and the picture of the building. I picked up the sticks and begin constructing some of the building. Sherri had a better understanding of what we were going to build. We made stick houses and then placed the people either on the outside or inside of the house doing different activities. She enjoyed that. This was a good exercise for both fine motor and communication skills. We discussed in sign and speech what the people were doing. If she did not mimic my sign, I moved her hands to do the right sign. I pointed to the picture, signed, and verbalized the action. Sherri enjoyed this plus it motivated her to learn. She became very excited when we built the stick houses and people. Making learning fun and exciting is an incentive for a person to learn and retain the material.

Coloring, first abstract pictures then pictures in coloring books, gave Sherri exercises in finger flexibility and dexterity. She enjoyed finger-painting. We also did fun finger exercises. Through these different exercises, she was then able to execute the signs easier.

With her gross motor skills, we took "fun" walks. We pointed, signed, and discovered various items in the environment. We consistently had special sessions each day on exercises for the gross and fine motor skills. These exercises were demonstrated to me by the physical and occupational therapists.

With self-help skills, I demonstrated proper ways to ensure good and expected hygiene for a teenager. Sherri mimicked these skills and then quickly included them independently into her daily routine. I also incorporated sign language and speech indicating the communication needed for these activities. Development of her skills in taking care of herself and her personal items were a top priority. Throughout all lessons, sign language was learned, retained, and used independently by Sherri.

A definite highlight for Sherri was the first time she went to a restaurant and went shopping with me. Sherri enjoyed getting dressed up and having her hair fixed. I showed her in a full-length mirror how beautiful she looked. I signed enthusiastically, "Beautiful." She was overjoyed. She was much different from the child who did not pay any attention to her looks or needs. Before we left for shopping, we made a list of items we wanted to buy. I cut out the picture of our intended purchases and the store where we would buy the item. I glued them on index cards. I pointed at a picture, signed, and said the name of the item. I then pointed at the picture of the store and signed, "We go store." Sherri mimicked the sign. I first manually guided her to sign the name of the item. I then pointed to the item and she signed independently. She was thrilled to be able to communicate what she wanted. She was able to match the picture of the store with the actual store.

While shopping, Sherri was very interested and curious about the names of various things. She learned quickly. After a short time, she was able to express herself and respond to questions.

I had pictures on index cards of the restaurant, inside and outside, where we were going to eat. She was familiar with the sign "eat," and she smiled. I then showed her the sign for "restaurant". I showed her many pictures of restaurants and signed, "Restaurant eat" as I pointed to each picture. Independently, she pointed to each picture and signed, "Restaurant eat." When we walked up to the front of the restaurant, she signed to me, "Restaurant eat." I smiled and signed, "Yes, restaurant eat." She behaved herself very appropriately. The menu had pictures and print of the types of food that were offered. She pointed to the picture, I signed, and she mimicked my sign. When the waitress arrived at our table, Sherri, with a big smile, pointed to the pictures, signed, and attempted to mouth the word. She was so proud that she could order by herself.

I, along with two other staff members of the Arizona Training Program, made arrangements to include Sherri in a group that we took to Disneyland. Even though there was reluctance from the other staff and the supervisor about having Sherri included in this group, Sherri was on her best behavior. She really enjoyed this special trip. This remarkable girl had made great strides which were way beyond people's expectations.

Sherri was a low-average intelligent girl locked up in her body. Once she was given the means and had a change of attitude toward "I Can," she improved miraculously. Because of both of us moving simultaneously, I lost contact with this extraordinary person. I heard from acquaintances that Sherri had become a young woman living alone. Her incredible progress was due to a strong family support, a belief in herself, and a belief in the "I Can" attitude.

By providing a person with a reason to progress and a want to succeed beyond the unreasonable expectations that have been placed upon them, they will be successful.

One preschooler, Donna, was autistic, speech and language-impaired, and had difficulty with physical mobility. Autism is a developmental disability. It affects both verbal and nonverbal communication. It also has a bearing upon an unwillingness to interact socially. They have difficulty in understanding people's feelings. They seem either very hyper or they can also manifest feelings of being very passive. They have repetitive movements like rocking back and forth. They may be over-sensitive to light, sound, smell, taste, or touch.[25]

Autism is difficult to diagnose or to develop a plan for. In the diagnosis of autism, the diagnostician needs a complete study of the medical and behavioral history and observation of the person in question. A possibility of other disabilities must be ruled out.

---

[25] Vogin, Gary, M.D. 5/22/2005. *Understanding Autism—Treatment*, http://aolsvc.health.webmd.aol.com/content/article/9/1680_54884.htm.

Having goals to gain an understanding of the environment helps the person with autism. With proper training, preferably by a specialist in autism, they can lose the characteristics of being autistic.

I worked with Donna in her home. She was oblivious to all people and most objects. Her family was quite concerned and willing to follow through on any suggestions which would benefit Donna. I began each session by sitting beside her. For the first two weeks, in a quiet voice and using sign language and speech, I would talk about her and me. Sign language attracted her and kept her attention. I would gently pick up her hand. If there was no resistance, I then glided her hand over my facial features. I continually told her my name. I let her feel my lips as I spoke. I was very conscious of using short, simple sentences or one- to two-word remarks. If Donna was resistant to my touch, I immediately took my hand away. After awhile, she began to acknowledge me by showing recognition through her facial expressions or body movements. I then compared the touch of my different facial features to hers. We began with just the nose. As we touched my nose, I said, "Nose." We then touched her nose and repeated the word. After a few times, this procedure became a game. Donna began to try and voice "nose." I then moved my head up and down, clapped lightly, and showed my excitement over her recognition. She seemed pleased when I reinforced her. We did this procedure with each facial part, using one facial part at a time but consistently reviewing the ones she had learned. Once she began showing recognition of our facial parts, both receptively and expressively, her mom joined us. I gently moved Donna's hand over my nose then said, "Nose." She mimicked. I then moved her had to her mom's nose and said, "Nose." Again, we used repetition with each facial part. She began independently recognizing facial features.

Donna had a favorite stuffed dog. I showed her the dog, we felt it. I had her feel the dog's nose and said, "Nose." She showed signs of recognition. She touched the dog's nose independently and verbalized "nose." I reinforced her by saying, "Yes," nodding my head, smiling, and clapping. Learning body parts aided in easier remediation of gross and fine motor skills. I consistently told her the name of the body part we were using. From then on, she began progressing. Even though the progression was slow, she began learning various items, including foods, clothes, and names of people and objects in her immediate environment. Donna eventually was able to verbalize her wants and needs.

The first attempt at verbalization without a speech or touch cue occurred on a day her mother was in the kitchen. She went to her and signed and tried to say "ice cream." This was the first day she communicated her wants. That day, she received ice cream from her pleasantly surprised mother. By the mother not giving up on Donna and believing in the "I Can" attitude, this young child began emerging from her private world.

A disorder which is similar to autism is Asperser's Syndrome. This syndrome appears between the ages of five and nine, which is later than autism. There are repetitive movements. Delays can be found in social interactions. They display no feelings in reaction to other people's situations. They speak and understand speech in just literal terms. They only speak of things that interest them. They continually respond or behave in a predictable manner. Problems with clumsiness exist. Unlike autism, this syndrome can last the length of a person's life.[26]They have average or above average intelligence.

When working or interacting with multiple disabilities, all programs must be coordinated. Consistency and presenting programs with a positive approach are the keys to progress in any type of remediation.

Multiple Sclerosis is a neurological, deteriorating disease. No one is absolutely sure of the cause of multiple sclerosis. Experts have studied an origin relating to the immune system cells which usually fight against diseases. The cells attack and damage myelin, which is the covering that protects the nerves. Nerve fibers called axons are exposed. This disease affects the spinal cord, the brain, and the nerves leading to the eye.

The attacks vary in intensity, frequency, and duration. The symptoms include muscle weakness, being overly fatigued, blurred vision, heat intolerance, inability to move tongue or jaw muscles causing slurred speech, and difficulties with mental functions and problems with incontinence exist. Normal daily activities like brushing one's teeth or combing one's hair can be very difficult and very tiring. Any type of activity which requires circular or repetitive movement is exhausting for someone with multiple sclerosis.

---

[26] http://users.wpi.edu/~trek/aspergers.html, June, 08, 2005, *Asperger's Syndrome*

Karen Johnson was at a university to obtain a degree as a chiropractor. During classes, she began having trouble focusing and her vision became blurry for periods of time. Frequently, her eyes would not focus together, giving her the feeling as if she was drunk. Often, Karen dropped her books or had a difficult time holding papers. Frequently, she would feel extremely hot and began sweating profusely. Her toes would begin dropping when she moved. She would begin scrapping her feet when walking. At times, Karen would be embarrassed because her mouth would sag and she would drool. At times, she had a difficult time speaking or thinking. A doctor diagnosed her with multiple sclerosis.

Despite being diagnosed with multiple sclerosis, Karen achieved her dream of becoming a chiropractor. But due to this disease, she was prevented from performing her job consistently. This was like having her feet pulled out from under her. Karen decided that even though she spent money and time to study in school, she would have to give up her dream of having a successful business as a chiropractor. The brutal consequences of this disease can be severe, but with a positive attitude, life's misfortunes can be positively challenged. Karen decided she would have to live with the fact that she had disabilities which would deny her the ability to work as a chiropractor. She moved to Arizona and began giving lectures for people interested in the areas of chiropractic medicine. She also was on an advisory committee for health problems.

Karen has now started an animal rescue clinic. Her main problem, both in being a chiropractor and being a leader in the animal rescue business, is having to cancel appointments because of her multiple sclerosis attacks. Some people or companies become very angry at her for canceling. If people would put themselves in her shoes, their attitudes would definitely change. Karen is a perfect model for the miraculous power of the "I Can" attitude.

When Karen has her multiple sclerosis attacks, she keeps quiet and comfortable. She sleeps several hours which helps her body relax and lessens the debilitating affects of multiple sclerosis. Her house just has tile on the floors. This helps build bone density when she walks. Because of her feeling very hot due to her disease, she needs to keep the air conditioner at a low temperature. Arizona gives her and her husband a tax break. She definitely has several ceiling fans in the house to circulate the air better. This remarkable woman has not given up. With the "I Can" attitude, she has achieved in many areas of life. For Karen, her sense of accomplishment is great. Despite having a debilitating disease, she continually strives to keep busy and active. On many occasions, she repeats to herself, "I Can." Through determination and the desire to succeed, Karen does succeed.

Mike Sherman was a graduate from Columbia Law School. He worked as a lawyer for an insurance company. He continually had weakness in his muscles and a feeling of overall tiredness. He felt at times as if he was standing on needles. Once in a while, he would temporarily lose his vision. He began going to many doctors. Each doctor felt his symptoms were caused by a viral infection.

Mike didn't actually realize the severity of his symptoms until he was in his thirties. He was at a Thanksgiving Parade with his young daughter. His young daughter was on his shoulders. His left eye began twitching and soon after, his right eye developed the same symptoms. He lost some of his vision. His shoulder began hurting and he became very weak. His mouth sagged. After that, he began researching his symptoms and researching various doctors. One doctor in Brooklyn told him that his symptoms and results of tests indicated that he had multiple sclerosis. Prednisone at high doses helped him to a degree. Interferon and betaseron, which are normally given to people afflicted with multiple sclerosis, helped him somewhat. Some time later, Mike developed leukemia which reduced the effectiveness of these drugs.

Mike Sherman's sense of humor, his attitude, and being stubborn kept him going. Sometimes, he found that it was very difficult to deal with his or his family's problems. During his attacks, he preferred to be left alone. That provided him the solitude to completely relax. This gave his body a chance to overcome the complete tiredness that he had felt.

Preceding an MS attack while in public, he would receive crude remarks about his physical appearance or his speech. Soon after an attack, a man made a comment about Mike being drunk. He told this inconsiderate man that he had multiple sclerosis. Another time, a stranger turned to Elinor Sherman, his wife, avoiding Mike completely, and asked if Mike could walk. With that, she told the man that Mike could speak and hear, so he should ask Mike himself. This is just another example of people questioning the disabled person's intellect.

When Mike Sherman moved to Arizona, he wanted to work at the same life insurance company he worked with back East. The management felt that because of his disabilities caused by multiple sclerosis attacks, he was no longer as effective as he could be. People need to have patience and understanding toward people with problems associated with a disability.

Mike eventually spoke with medical students on the effects of multiple sclerosis. Through this, Mike was able to help people with this debilitating disease receive better care.

Mike Sherman's story is another example that one can survive despite mounting obstacles with love and support from family and the "I Can" attitude.

Muscular dystrophy is a genetic disease. The characteristic of the disease is a continual deterioration of the skeletal muscles. These muscles control movement. When the muscle fibers weaken, they are replaced by fatty fibrous tissues.[26] During times of weakness of the facial and neck muscles, difficulty in swallowing will occur.

There are many types of muscular dystrophy. Types are dependent upon age of onset and which muscles are affected. One or more muscles weaken and degenerate. There are three that are the most common. These are Duchenne, facioscapulohumeral, and myotonic.[27]

---

[26] Burtner, Paul, DMD. 2004. *Oral Health Care for Persons with Disabilities.* June 1, 2005. From *http://www.dental.ufl.edu/Faculty/Pburtner/ disabilities/English/phmysdys.htm*

The onset of Duchenne occurs between the ages of two to six years old. The muscles of the limbs and trunk first become weak and then wasted.

Facioscapulohumeral can begin from either childhood or early adulthood. Facial muscles are affected.

Myotonic appears between childhood and middle age. Face, feet, hands, and neck have generalized weakness and muscle wasting.

All separate disorders are divided into two categories— atrophy and dystrophy. Atrophy is the cause of muscle wasting which comes about from another disorder that begins in the nerve system resulting from the inability to use muscles. Dystrophy is "the wasting of the muscles from within themselves."[28]

Persons who experience characteristics of muscular dystrophy should contact a personal physician. If necessary, the physician can refer the person to a muscular dystrophy clinic. To locate a clinic in a specific area, call the headquarters in Tucson, Arizona (520)-529-2000 or (800) 572-1717.

The muscular dystrophy clinics provide a team approach to diagnosing muscular dystrophy and determining the follow-up programs.[29] The diagnostic procedures focus on clinical examinations, family history, electromyogram measurements of

---

[27] Muscular Dystrophy Association. *Muscular Dystrophy Services. 2004. pp 4-5*

[28] Disability Resource Network of BC. 5-18-2005. *Neurological Disabilities— Muscular Dystrophy*. 6-8-2005. p.3-4 of 6

electrical activity for muscles, serum enzyme tests which measure the amount of muscle protein, genetic tests, and a muscle biopsy.

The follow-up programs focus on managing the disorder: physical, occupational, respiratory and speech therapy, interaction with personal physicians, genetic counseling, support groups, flu inoculations, and transportation.

The Muscular Dystrophy Association also provides services for repairs and modifications for wheelchairs, leg braces, and communication devices.

Communication for people who have multiple disabilities along with a physical impairment can be a special challenge. Sign language or speech may be difficult because of specific muscle weaknesses. Augmentative or alternative communication uses a specialized approach. This method uses pictures or symbols, or print on a paper supported by a board and a pointer if needed. Specialized computers are now being used. Information on the computer can be pictographic or print. Some computers are voice synthesized. Through these products, a person with multiple disabilities has a method of communicating and interacting with friends, family, and colleagues.

People who are deaf-blind experience a different encounter with their environment than seeing and hearing people do. People who can see and hear have the ability to deal with everyday experiences as they happen. The ability to cope with

---

[29] Muscular Dystrophy Association. 2004. *MDA Services-Individual, Family, and Community.* 6-10-05. pp.18-25.

life experiences for the deaf-blind individual is dependent upon his educational, transitional, and life training skills. A major factor in adaptability is the age the sensory deficits occurred. With teamwork of all agencies and specialists, rehabilitation services and education, the deaf-blind individual can progress and succeed in different areas of life.

Without training, education, and support, a person who is deaf-blind could experience social isolation, problems with communication, trouble with motivation, difficulty with concept development, and a struggle with interactions.

Support from caregivers and loved ones can make a difference with whether the deaf-blind person succeeds and progresses.

People with multiple disabilities and their caregivers must be cautious of providing, promoting, and following good nutrition and wellness programs. Because of physical limitations, the person with multiple disabilities must participate in an interdisciplinary program for health and wellness. Lack of exercise and complications from combining certain medications or the long-term use of medications can be factors in creating additional dental, physical, or mental problems.

Consistent participation from all household members with the follow-up of all programs will ensure a comfortable and a more self-gratifying lifestyle for the person with multiple disabilities. Promoting the "I Can" attitude will enable a person to master many challenges in life and foster independence.

ADDITIONAL REFERENCES

Organizations

Muscular Dystrophy
Association
3300 East Sunrise Drive
Tucson, AZ 85718-3299

Phone: 800-572-1717

520-259-2000
Email: www.mdausa.org
Fax: 520-529-5300

National Rehabilitation
Information Center
4200 Forbes Boulevard, Suite
202
Lanham, MD 20706

Phone: 800-346-2742
Web: www.naric.com

National Institute of
Neurological Disorders and
Stroke
 PO Box 5801
Bethesda, MD 20824

Phone 800-352-9424
301-496-3285

American Association of the
Deaf-Blind
814 Thayer Ave, Ste. 302
Silver Spring, MD 20910

TTY: 301-588-6545
Fax: 301-588-8705

Helen Keller National Center
for Deaf-Blind Youth and
Adults
111 Middle Neck Road
Sands Point, NY 11050-1299

Phone: 516-944-8900

TTY: 516-944-8637
Fax: 516-944-7302

PERIODICALS AND NEWSLETTERS

TASH Newsletter
29 W. Susquehanna Avenue,
Suite 210
Baltimore, MD 21204

Phone: 410-828-8274
TTY: 410-828-1306
Email: www.tash.org

DB-Link
Overview on Deaf-Blindness
345 N. Monmouth Ave.
Monmouth, OR 97361

Phone: 800-438-9376
TTY: 800-854-7013
Fax: 503-838-8150
Email: dblink@tr.wosc.osshe.
edu

BOOKS

Including Students with Severe and Multiple Disabilities in Typical Classrooms: Practical Strategies for Teachers

Downing, J.E.

Educating Children with Multiple Disabilities: Transdisciplinary Approach

Orelove, F.
Sobsey, D.

Augmentative and Alternative Communication

Shane, Howard
Sauer, Maggie

The Deaf-blind/Severely Profoundly Handicapped Child

Anderson, S.

Therapeutic Claims in Multiple Sclerosis

Sibley, W. and others

Legwork: An Inspiring Journey Through A Chronic Illness

MacFarlane, E.B.
Burstein, P.

Chapter VII

LEGAL AND MORAL RIGHTS FOR PEOPLE WITH DISABILITIES

People with disabilities are stigmatized because they use a variety of methods to communicate, may have a lack of understanding about various concepts, use various equipment and methods for mobility, or they may behave differently or possibly approach life in a different manner using diverse methods. Nevertheless, people with disabilities are people, too. They deserve respect and have the same rights that everyone else has in a society. Instead of being hesitant to interact with people with disabilities, include them in daily life experiences. People can learn from one another despite their differences. People learning from each other can be rewarding. I have learned many wonderful ideas and concepts from people with many different types of disabilities. I have learned not to critique people but enjoy and relish what they say or do. I have learned the importance of being patient with all people. I take the time to share with each person I encounter as each person is an individual.

Words in our language, both in writing and speaking, can be very powerful. What people read or hear can be influential in their thinking and in their mannerisms. The media—television, movies, newspapers, video games, and radio—can have a major impact upon a person's life. If a person hears derogatory words or phrases enough times, his subconscious mind will process those belittling words. The words will become ingrained in the mind. This results in a low self-image for many people with disabilities.

The affect of parents' actions and language can sway their child to respond in a certain way. Parents mold their children's minds to learn from or to discriminate against races, nationalities, languages, or disabilities. In schools, children call each other "retard" to demean each other. Many of these misinformed children have heard their guardians use that word in a derogatory manner. Upon hearing the word "retard," the child who has mental retardation suffers a terrible blow to his ego.

Today, many parents allow their children to view television, movies, video games, or listen to the radio without supervision. Words and themes are not censored in many movies and television programs. Children, as well as adults, often mimic what they have seen or heard. Opening discussions with the whole family, loved ones, or friends will help separate reality from fantasy, especially concerning disabilities.

When counseling family members of individuals with disabilities, I encouraged group discussions. I began to see marked improvement in all family members when family group discussions were instigated. After asking, researching, and discussing problems or questions, all family members were able to relate better with each other and handle the stresses of having a family member with disabilities.

The lack of understanding toward people with disabilities can lead to vicious myths and rumors. When meeting a person with disabilities, treat them no differently than people who do not have disabilities. Shake hands. Ask appropriate questions about them. Speak about topics that are usually spoken about, such as current events both in the community and the world, and of likes and dislikes of each individual in the conversational group. While speaking, use a normal speaking tone. Some people tend to speak to a person with disabilities as if they were a very young child or as if they did not understand the language that was used. They over-exaggerate words and speak in simplistic terms. Speak to a person at their age level.

People must be cautious of the terminology that is used when a person with disabilities is spoken of or spoken to.[30] Do not refer to a person as being handicapped or disabled. Handicap refers to either an "environmental barrier" or an "attitudinal barrier." Instead of saying "disabled," use the phrase "person with disabilities." Do not use the term "retard;" say a "person with mental retardation." Avoid using terms like "suffers from cerebral palsy;" use instead, "a

---

[30] Dept. of the Secretary of State of Canada. http://www.schoolnet.ca/aboriginal/disabl12. June 2005. *Way Of Words*. Minister of Supply and Services, Canada. 1991. p. 1-3 of 5.

person with cerebral palsy." Instead of saying "a person is deaf and dumb" or "the person suffers a hearing loss," say "a person who is deaf/hard of hearing or has a hearing impairment." By restating, it designates that the person is not a condition, but an individual.[31]

When referring to disabilities, do <u>not</u> use the common words such as special, inadequate, incompetent, or words which indicate that they are a separate group from the rest of society.

The use of the word "normal" in reference to a person indicates that a person with disabilities is not normal.

Dennis, an acquaintance who is totally blind, would become amused when people became flustered when they asked him, "Did you see….?" He would turn around and say amusingly, "No, I am blind!" Another person, John, is a friend who has a hearing impairment. He would laugh when people suddenly realized that they had used the phrase, "Did you hear that …?" These words are part of the English language. There is no reason to worry or be cautious of using these words.

Facial expressions, eye movements, and body language can relate tactless messages just as much as the spoken word. Because of my pronunciation of words and jumbling up of the word order when I am tired, I have noticed insulting looks from people. They raise their eyebrows, smile a little, and shift their position. Many times, I have had people turn to a companion and ask them what I had said. If a person does not understand what a person with disabilities has expressed, do <u>not</u> turn to their companion and

----

[31] idem, p. 2 of 5.

question what the person said. If in doubt of what is being said, take the time to ask the person with disabilities to repeat what they had said. Do not insult them by questioning somebody else.

Along with the use of a different terminology, being cautious of body language is extremely important. Body language, especially facial expressions, can tell a person's true feelings. On outings with people with disabilities, they have questioned why somebody is looking at them in a disrespectful manner or pointing at them. Showing respect to each person regardless of their mental or physical capabilities will ensure a more caring society and will aid in the development of every person.

In addition to a better awareness of the moral rights for the person with disabilities, the intensification of legal rights has increased the productivity and acceptability of persons with disabilities in our society.

On July 26, 1990, Congress passed the **Americans with Disabilities ACT** (ADA). ADA forbids discrimination against people with disabilities in "employment, state and local governments, public accommodations, commercial facilities, transportation, and telecommunications."[32]

The titles in this law increase the opportunities for people with disabilities. For this law to apply, a person must have a physical or mental disability that limits one or more of life's activities, or be either a person who has a record of such disabilities or is seen by

---

[32] U.S. Dept of Justice, June 05, *A Guide to Disability Rights Laws August 2004.*

other people as having a disability. The titles of the Americans with Disabilities Act are as follows:

Title I states that discrimination against qualified people with disabilities is unlawful. It forbids discrimination in the following areas: hiring, training, promotions, pay, and other areas of employment. This title also states that employers need to adjust work areas to accommodate any physical or mental disabilities. It also prohibits any questions about disabilities prior to a job offer. For any complaints or information about this title call, 800-669-4000 (voice) or 800-669-6820 (TTY).[33] **Title II** requires all agencies within the state and local governments not to discriminate against people with disabilities in any services, programs, and activities. Once the person with disabilities is hired, specific architectural guidelines must be implemented to allow the person with disabilities to do their job without any barriers. This title allows provisions for people who have hearing, vision, or speech impairments. Programs must be relocated if the work provisions prevent accurate communication for people with hearing, vision, or speech impairments.

Another section of this title concerns public transportation. Compliance to this law will require public transportation services to have accessible vehicles for people with disabilities. If adjustments are cost prohibitive, then paratransit services will be enacted. For a paratransit system, it stipulates that if a person with physical or mental impairments cannot use the public transit system, then they

---

[33] idem, p. 3 of 15.

can be picked up and taken to their destinations. For questions or concerns call 888-446-4511 (Voice and Relay).[34]

Title III covers public accommodation. This title prevents discrimination of persons with disabilities for them to have the right to use and enjoy public accommodations and public facilities such as "restaurants, retail stores, hotels, movie theaters, private schools, convention centers, doctor's offices, homeless shelters, transportation depots, zoos, funeral homes, daycare centers, and recreation facilities including sports and fitness clubs."[35] All these facilities must have accessibility for people with physical disabilities. They also are required to have required provisions for communication for people who require different means to communicate—people with hearing, speech, and vision impairment. For any questions or concerns, call 888-225-5322 (Voice) or 888-835-5322 (TTY).[36]

Title IV is the Telecommunications Relay Services. This title stipulates that the person with hearing impaired disabilities and speech or language disabilities will have the availability of telecommunication services twenty-four hours a day and seven days a week. For any questions or concerns, call 888-225-5322 (Voice) or 835-5322 (TTY).[37]

The **Telecommunications Act** dictates that all equipment in telecommunication services is available and usable for people

---

[34] idem p. 4 of 15

[35] idem p. 5 of 15.

[36] idem p. 6 of 15.

[37] idem p. 6 of 15.

with disabilities. This act stipulates that people with disabilities will be able to obtain "products and services such as telephones, cell phones, pagers, call-waiting, and operator services."[38] For any questions or concerns, call 888-225-5322 (voice) or 835-5322 (TTY).

Fair Housing Act states that a person with disabilities cannot be denied selling or renting a house solely based upon the disabilities. This act also states that an owner or landlord must allow reasonable exceptions to a person with disabilities that require certain housing modifications for their disabilities. If a person with physical disabilities needs to enlarge door spaces so that he can comfortably maneuver in a wheelchair, he will be allowed to make the changes in his living space as long as he pays for the costs.

This act requires that in new multifamily housing with three or more family units, the units must be accessible for persons with multiple disabilities. This includes door spaces being wide enough for wheelchairs to enter. Also, the kitchen and bathrooms must be wide enough for a person using a wheelchair to comfortably maneuver. For any questions or concerns on The Fair Housing Act, call 800-669-9777 (voice) and 800-927-9275 (TTY).[39]

Air Carrier Access Act makes allowances for people who have physical or mental disabilities. This act requires assistance in boarding. Newly built airport facilities must have accessibility

---

[38] idem p. 7 of 15.
[39] idem p. 8 of 15.

features for the person with disabilities. For any questions or concerns, call 202-366-2220 (voice) and 202-366-0511 (TTY).[40]

Voting Accessibility for the Elderly and Handicapped Act mandates that all polling places be accessible to the elderly and persons with disabilities for federal elections. If there is no location available, an alternative means for voting must be rendered. TTY's or TDD's (telecommunication devices for the deaf) for the people with hearing-impairment must be available. For any questions or concerns call 800-253-3931 (Voice and TTY).[41]

National Voter Registration Act of 1993 known as the "Motor Voter Act" is enacted to encourage persons who are minorities or persons who have disabilities to vote. This mandates that all offices of state-funded programs provide services which provide "applicants with voter registration forms," help with filling out the appropriate forms, and hand over the forms to the appropriate state official. Any questions or concerns contact 800-253-3931 (Voice and TTY).[42]

Civil Rights of Institutionalized Persons Act gives the U.S. attorney general the right to inspect facilities that confine people. These facilities include both state and local facilities. These are "prisons, jails, pretrial detention centers, juvenile correction facilities, publicly operated nursing homes, and institutions for people with psychiatric or developmental disabilities." This law gives the attorney general the right to investigate the health and

---

[40] idem p. 8 of 15.
[41] p. 9 of 15.
[42] p. 9 of 15.

safety of all people in the aforementioned places. The attorney general cannot investigate one individual but investigates the rights of all residents in a facility. For any questions or concerns contact 877-218-5228 (Voice and TTY).[43]

The **Rehabilitation Act** prevents discrimination of any person with disabilities in programs which are components of federal agencies, programs which receive federal assistance, or programs that have federal employment.

Under the Rehabilitation Act, there are four sections—501, 503, 504, and 508.[44]

Section 501 stipulates that it is mandatory to have affirmative action and no discrimination against people with disabilities in employment by federal agencies.

Section 503 stipulates affirmative action and disallows discrimination by federal government contractors with contracts of more than $10,000.

Section 504 affirms that no persons with disabilities in the United States should be ostracized or penalized from any programs which receive federal assistance or executive agencies.

Section 508 institutes regulations for electronic and information technology which is developed and regulated by the federal government. The federal electronic and information technology is available for the use of public citizens and employees of the federal government.

---

[43] p. 10 of 15.
[44] idem p. 11-13 of 25.

Individuals with Disabilities Education Act (IDEA) obligates all public schools to enroll children regardless of their disabilities. Public schools must provide "a free appropriate public education in the least restrictive environment." This law has been interpreted in many school districts to place all children with disabilities in a public classroom regardless of mental or physical disabilities. This is called inclusion. The special education teacher is allotted a certain amount of time to help each student with disabilities in the classroom. There are a few schools for specific problems such as a school for the deaf or blind, detention centers, jails, or mental institutions. However, these students are involved in the inclusion system as soon as possible. In all areas, students with disabilities can be taken out of the classroom for speech, occupational therapy, physical therapy, and counseling.

Wherever a student with disabilities is educated, there must be an Individual Education Plan (I.E.P.) developed which states the objectives that will be followed throughout the year and then reviewed. The process for this begins with screening and identification by the school psychologist. If a child has a need for special education, then a consent for evaluation and procedural safeguard notice is given to the legal guardian to sign. The initial evaluation and eligibility determination is completed by the school psychologist. The special education teacher may be asked to give a few tests. The I.E.P. is then written by a team of people who have knowledge of the student's academic, behavioral, psychological, social, and emotional aspects. Also included in this are the physical skills, speech patterns, organizational patterns, and self-help skills.

Both the negative and positive areas are evaluated. The team includes parents or legal guardians, the special education teacher, the school psychologist, the classroom teacher, physical therapists, speech therapists, occupational therapists, the principal, the special education director, and any other person or agency involved with the student with disabilities. If a parent or guardian wants anybody else to be included in this team, they have the legal right.

Through this meeting, the student will be placed in an environment which coincides with the least restrictive environment. Legal guardians must sign consent for initial placement. The guardians will be provided with a prior written notice; then the student will be placed. There are semi and annual reviews of the I.E.P. At annual meetings, a new I.E.P. is written. Every three years, it is required that the team will meet again to evaluate the progress. If the student has met all needs, then there is a possibility of program termination.

In a small town I worked in, one foster mother who had legal jurisdiction over a young boy with multiple disabilities brought her lawyer to the I.E.P. meeting. Even though the objectives were supported by test or data from consistent observation, the foster mother's expectations of needs were totally different than the professional staff's. For approximately five hours, the team discussed various objectives that could satisfy all team members. I.E.Ps cannot be instigated until all persons on the team agree and sign off on it. The legal guardian is the prime person that must sign the I.E.P.

When I was a mental retardation specialist in the institution for people with mental retardation, we had to write Individual Personal Plans (I.P.P.). After testing and compiling data from observation, all people concerned with the welfare of the person with mental retardation wrote objectives for the I.P.P. The objectives covered self-help skills, independent living skills, social skills, behavior skills, physical therapy, occupational therapy, counseling, and academics. These objectives needed to be signed by all professionals involved, including the legal guardians. When a person is placed in an institution, it is sometimes very difficult to locate the legal guardians. All means possible were made to locate the guardians. If guardians could not be located, then people appointed by the court were sent in place of the guardians.

When I worked as a parent advisor for youngsters who were birth to five years old, the coordinator tested and wrote a report indicating negative and positive aspects of the child. Communication, self-help, perceptional, auditory, visual, physical, gross and fine motor skills, and mental needs were written for the child. The objectives were usually based upon communication, self-help skills, auditory and visual perception, fine and gross motor skills. The responsibility of the legal guardians was to agree to the objectives and follow the plans throughout the week. The majority of the guardians followed the objectives. The babies progressed if the legal guardians followed the objectives written.

The **Head Start** program is a federally funded pre-school program. This program is for both low-income families and preschoolers with disabilities. Even though this program is optional, it is very important for the early childhood development of communication, mobility, fine and gross motor skills, self-help, socialization, and visual and auditory perception. Individual Family Service Plans (I.F.S.P.) are written. I.F.S.P. follows the same guidelines as I.E.P.

All programs and laws offered from the federal, state, and city governments and people's change in attitudes toward people with disabilities enable each person, regardless of mental or physical capabilities, to live together in harmony.

ADDITIONAL REFERENCES

Organizations

U.S. Department of Justice
Civil Rights Division
950 Pennsylvania Avenue, N.W.
Disability Rights Section—NYAV
Washington, D.C. 20530

Office of Civil Rights

800-514-0301 (Voice)
800-514-0383 (TTY)

888-446-4511 (Voice/
TTY)

Federal Transit AdministrationEmail:
400 Seventh Street, S.W. Room 9102

Washington, D.C. 20590

Email:
www.fla.dot.gov/
transit_data_info/ada

Federal Communications Commission
445 12th Street, S.W.
Washington, D.C. 20554

888-225-5322 (Voice)
888-835-5322 (TTY)

Office of Program Compliance and
Disability Rights
Office of Fair Housing and Equal
Opportunity
U.S. Department of Housing and
Urban Dev.
451 7th St., S.W., Room 5242
Washington, D.C. 20410

800-669-9777 (Voice)

Office of Special Education Program
Office of Special Education and
Rehabilitative Services
U.S. Department of Education
400 Maryland Avenue, S.W.
Washington, D.C. 20202-7100

202-205-5507
(Voice/TTY)

Arizona Center for Disability Law   602-274-6287 (Voice/
                                           TTY)
3839 N. Third St., Suite 209 Fax: 602-
274-6779
Phoenix, Arizona 85012

ARTICLES

At http://www.socialsecurityhome.com, there are several articles on the law and disabilities.

"Disability Law"
SSDI Insurance Qualifications

"SSI for Children"
Supplemental Security Income

"Fibromyalgia Disability"
SSDI Insurance

"Disability Act"
Supplemental Security Income

"Disability Lawyers"
Definition of Disability

"SSI Application"
Disability Benefits

"How to Apply for Disability"
SS Disability

"SSI Eligibility"
How does SS Determine if Someone is Disabled

BOOKS

Special Needs Trust Administration Manual: A Guide for Trustees — Barbara D. Jackins

Voices from the Edge: Narratives About the American with Disabilities Act — Rogers M. Smith, Ruth O'Brien (Editor)

Make Them Go Away: Clint Eastwood and Christopher Reeve and the Case Against Disability Rights — Mary Johnson

Federal Disability Law in a Nutshell — Bonnie Poitras Tucker

Accommodations in Higher Education Under the ADA: A No-Nonsense Guide for Clinicians Educators, Administrators, and Lawyers — Michael Gordon, Shelby Keiser

The Law of Disability and The Legal Professional — Jeffrey Scott Wolfe, Lisa Proszak

The Law of Disability Discrimination	Ruth Colker Bonnie Tucker
Disability, Difference, Discrimination	Anita Silvers
Americans with Disabilities Practice And Compliance Manual	Trenkner, T.R

www.ingramcontent.com/pod-product-compliance
Lightning Source LLC
Chambersburg PA
CBHW061253280526
45784CB00002B/753